KV-144-457

SILICON LITERACIES
Communication, Innovation and Education in the Electronic Age
Edited by Ilana Snyder

AFRICAN AMERICAN LITERACIES
Elaine Richardson

LITERACY IN THE NEW MEDIA AGE
Gunther Kress

F ЭТ   Г

"In this complex and engaging study, Elaine Richardson unravels the history, importance, vivacity, and complexity of Hiphop discourse practices in pop culture. From Jamaica's Dancehall DJs and yardies, German Hiphop artists, gamers, and more, Elaine Richardson demonstrates that as Hiphop expands throughout the globe, it continues to spread and incorporate African American aesthetics and language ideology. *Hiphop Literacies* is required reading for those interested in understanding the complex relationship between Hiphop, popular culture, and the African American language ideology."

Marcyliena Morgan, *Stanford University, US*

Hiphop Literacies is an exploration of the rhetorical language and literacy practices of African Americans, with a focus on the Hiphop generation. Richardson analyzes the lyrics and discourse of Hiphop, explodes myths and stereotypes about Black culture and language and shows how Hiphop language is a global ambassador of the English language and American culture.

In locating rap and Hiphop discourse within a trajectory of Black discourses, Richardson examines African American Hiphop in secondary oral contexts such as rap music, song lyrics, electronic and digital media, oral performances and cinema.

Hiphop Literacies brings together issues and concepts that are explored in the disciplines of folklore, ethnomusicology, sociolinguistics, discourse studies and New Literacies Studies.

Elaine Richardson is Associate Professor of English and Applied Linguistics at Pennsylvania State University. She is the author of *African American Literacies* (Routledge, 2003) and co-editor of *Understanding African American Rhetoric: Classical Origins to Contemporary Innovations* (Routledge, 2003).

LITERACIES

Series Editor: David Barton

Lancaster University

Literacy practices are changing rapidly in contemporary society in response to broad social, economic and technological changes: in education, the workplace, the media and in everyday life. This series reflects the burgeoning research and scholarship in the field of literacy studies and its increasingly interdisciplinary nature. The series aims to provide a home for books on reading and writing which consider literacy as a social practice and which situate it within broader institutional contexts. The books develop and draw together work in the field; they aim to be accessible, interdisciplinary and international in scope, and to cover a wide range of social and institutional contexts.

CITY LITERACIES

Learning to Read Across Generations and Cultures

Eve Gregory and Ann Williams

LITERACY AND DEVELOPMENT

Ethnographic Perspectives

Edited by Brian V. Street

SITUATED LITERACIES

Theorising Reading and Writing in Context

Edited by David Barton, Mary Hamilton and Roz Ivanic

MULTILITERACIES

Literacy Learning and the Design of Social Futures

Edited by Bill Cope and Mary Kalantzis

GLOBAL LITERACIES AND THE WORLD-WIDE WEB

Edited by Gail E. Hawisher and Cynthia L. Selfe

STUDENT WRITING

Access, Regulation, Desire

Theresa M. Lillis

HIPHOP LITERACIES

Elaine Richardson

Routledge
Taylor & Francis Group

LONDON AND NEW YORK

First published 2006
by Routledge
2 Park Square, Milton Park, Abingdon, Oxon OX14 4RN

Simultaneously published in the USA and Canada
by Routledge
270 Madison Ave, New York, NY 10016

Routledge is an imprint of the Taylor and Francis Group, an informa business

© 2006 Elaine Richardson

Typeset in Baskerville by Keystroke, 28 High Street, Tettenhall, Wolverhampton
Printed and bound in Great Britain by TJ International Ltd, Padstow, Cornwall

British Library Cataloguing in Publication Data
A catalogue record for this book is available from the British Library

Library of Congress Cataloguing in Publication Data
Richardon, Elaine B., 1960–
   Hiphop literacies /by Elaine Richardson.
      p. cm.
   ISBN 0–415–32928–0 (hardback) — ISBN 0–415–32927–2 (pbk.)
   1. African Americans—Languages. 2. English language—United States—
   Rhetoric. 3. English language—Social aspects—United States.
   4. Hip-hop—United States. 5. Black English—United States.
   6. Americanisms. I. Title.

PE3102.N42R52 2006
427'.97308996073—dc22   2006001066

         ISBN10: 0–415–32928–0 (hbk)
         ISBN10: 0–415–32927–2 (pbk)
         ISBN10: 0–203–39110–1 (ebk)

         ISBN13: 978–0–415–32928–6 (hbk)
         ISBN13: 978–0–415–32927–9 (pbk)
         ISBN13: 978–0–203–39110–5 (ebk)

CONTENTS

ILLUSTRATIONS

Figures

Tables

ACKNOWLEDGEMENTS

First giving honor to my creator for making me and giving me the parents and foreparents that I have. Every book I write will always be dedicated to them, especially my mama and daddy, and to my beautiful daughters—Booniqua, Rock, and Bokie a.k.a. Evelyn, Ebony and Kaila. Thank you for your encouragement and kind words about how smart Mommy is. It really helps me to know that you think what I do is important.

Many people have helped me, including mentors, colleagues, students, and friends: my queen and mentor, Dr. Geneva Smitherman for her scholarship, example and constant support and inspiration; Dr. Carolyn Cooper, my Jamaican sistren, of the University of the West Indies, Department of Literatures in English, without whom I would not have had the opportunity to teach and do research as Fulbright Scholar at UWI during Fall, 2004. Dr. Velma Pollard, another queen of Jamaica, poet, teacher and scholar of Rastafarian Language. Dr. Pollard's conversations, insight and feedback on Jamaican and African American cross-culturality have been invaluable; Dr. Peter Patrick, mi bredrin, of the University of Essex, sociolinguist and scholar of creole linguistics provided valuable criticisms and suggestions; Dr. Jannis Androutsopoulos, my German connection, Institut für Deutsche Sprache, has been very generous and cooperative, providing guidance and criticism in German linguistics and Hiphop scholarship; my colleagues, Drs. Gwendolyn Pough of Women's Studies and Writing at Syracuse University, Adam Banks also of Syracuse's Writing Program, and Dr. Rebecca Rogers of Washington University of St. Louis who all read and commented upon certain portions of this work, also Dr. Gabriella Appel of Penn State University; Dr. Carol Myers-Scotton, expert contact linguist, whose work and commentary I found invaluable in heightening my understanding of German incorporation of African American language. Nuff thanks to my West Indian brothers, Dr. Cary Fraser of History and African/African American Studies at Penn State, for critical commentary on Jamaican–African American crossings, and Dr. John Rickford of Stanford University, leading expert in Afro diasporic linguistics, creolistics, and sociolinguistics. I owe thanks also to my Jamaican cultural studies scholar and sisterfriend, Dr. Sonjah Stanley-Niaah, for feedback and immense collegiality. I must also thank my students and friends at Penn State University who shared their video game expertise with me—Mr. Kevin Browne, Durell Kvasny, and Dorrian Carraway. Dr. Mark Anthony Neal of Duke University, prolific scholar of Black popular culture, music, and masculinity provided valuable insights. I also extend shout outs to colleagues at various conferences where I've presented aspects of this work while in progress: Conference on College Composition and Communication (CCCCs); Feminism(s) and Rhetoric(s); New Ways of Analyzing Variation (NWAV). Big Ups to Isabelle of the Stanford ALL project and Dr. Robin Queen of University of Michigan for excellent suggestions on German Hiphop, also Dr.Ulrich Miethaner. Shouts to Dr. Gwendolyn Pough, Dr. Vershawn Young, Dr. David Holmes, Dr. Wendy Sharer, Dr. Vorris Nunley, Ms. Beverly Silverstein and Dr. Linda Tucker for inviting me to Syracuse, Iowa, Pepperdine, East Carolina, and Arkansas, respectively, to present aspects of this work while in progress.

Big Ups to the vast numbers of people who care about Hiphop and Black youth that I have met at Hiphop conferences: Cleveland (Rock Hall and Cleveland State University Hiphop Conference); Madison, Wisconsin (Hiphop as a Movement); Newark, New Jersey (National Political Hiphop Convention); Hiphop Feminism (Conference at University of Chicago). My online Hiphop brother—Brotha Rushay representin for South African Hiphop; One Love to all of di Jamaican posse dem and Hiphop crews from Logwood Hanover to Kingston to Brooklyn, Billy B, Cutta Jack, Element, Mahlon, Chris Bryan, Stevie G, Big Ev, Rock, my play dawta Ev, my Penn State students, and all of my UWI students who shared their Knowledge, Wisdom and Ovah standin. To my friend and mentor Brotha Docta Keith Gilyard and his lovely wife, my girlfriend to the end, Sharyn Gilyard for havin a sista's back! Penn State colleagues Drs. Sinfree Makoni, Karen Johnson, Cheryl Glenn, Lovalerie King, Iyun Osagie, Avis Kuhns, Deborah Atwater, Christine Clark Evans, Ron Jackson, and Linda Selzer; NCTE Black Caucus; national colleagues whose work upon which I draw inspiration and influence—Drs. Denise Troutman, Marcyliena Morgan, Imani Perry, Felicia Miyakawa, CeCe Cutler, Mary Bucholz and Dr. Jim Gee. Also, to the entire It's Bigger Than Hip Hop Posse—Alim, Pennycook, Sarkar, Ibrahim, Yasin, Newman.

Much love and respect to the globetrotting Alexandra Jenkins for translations of German Hiphop websites and for sharing her knowledge of the Berlin Hiphop scene. A Big thank you to Sara-Eve Rivera for permission to reproduce her wonderful drawings of Lil' Kim, Foxy Brown, and Eko Fresh. Thanks to past research assistants Aesha Adams, Chaunda McDavis, Melvette Melvin Davis, and, especially, Tony Ceraso for a whole bunch a stuff!

For permission to use small excerpts from the lyrics of Lil' Kim, I thank Alfred Publishing Company for the following two songs:

LIL' DRUMMER BOY
By KIMBERLY JONES, SEAN PUFFY COMBS,
MARIO WINANS,
T. BURTON and REGGIE NOBLE

I would also like to acknowledge the support of Routledge in the persons of Louisa Semlyen, Elizabeth Johnston, Lauren McGraw, Matt Byrnie, Kate Ahl, Sarah DeVos and Ursula Mallows.

Aspects of the research for this book were funded by: the Africana Research Center, Pennsylvania State University, Dr. Beverly Vandiver, Director; the Center for Language Acquisition, Pennsylvania State University, Dr. James Lantolf, Director; Minority Faculty Development Funds, Pennsylvania State University, Dr. James Stewart, Senior Faculty Mentor; Pennsylvania State University Research Graduate Studies Office, Dr. Ray Lombra. Without such assistance this work could not possibly have been developed into its present form.

Any shortcomings are entirely my own.

PREFACE

In an article entitled "Hip Hop Hogwash in the Schools," Michelle Malkin goes to great lengths to discredit efforts by educators to incorporate aspects of Hiphop culture in their curricula by exploring its intellectual foundations from the perspectives of their various disciplines. Her research into the matter seems restricted to what she could learn from the web. There she found my syllabus for a course that bears the name of this book. She writes: "And at Pennsylvania State University, I discovered, students were required to attend a 'Mos Def Concert' and write 'a page concerning Hip Hop Literacies that you observe at the performance.' Also mandatory: in-class listening sessions of 'old school rap' and in-class 'viewing of various female rapper's (*sic*) videos.'" (http://www.vdare.com/malkin/hiphop. htm) Okay, so I had a typo in my syllabus. But that was the least of her concerns. Her main problem was with the content—Hiphop as a valid subject of study. Needless to say, Malkin is hardly alone. She is one of scores of people who see incorporation of popular culture or diverse perspectives into the curriculum as dumbing down and as a waste of time. What I strive to do in this book is show the depth, the importance, and the immediate necessity of acknowledging one of the most contemporary, accessible, and contentious of African American literacies, Hiphop literacies.

Seminal work in studies of literacy by scholars such as Goody and Watt (1968) and Ong (1982/2002) focused on a "great divide" that exists between literates and those who have been untouched by literate culture. In this view, literacy restructures thought and is a print-bound, autonomous, private, mental, context-free activity. Over the past few decades, the field of literacy studies has taken a social multi-modal turn as is exemplified in the New Literacy Studies (NLS), which promote the idea that literacy must be conceived of more broadly, as ideological, not print bound, and socially constructed. Furthermore, oral memory and knowledge-making systems are connected to literate ones. As Ong himself argues, literacy cannot be divorced from orality. Another school of thought in the New Literacy Studies explores the many types of literacy—visual and sonic, to name just two. Within visual literacy there are different ways to read, for example, music videos on MTV, video games, websites, or billboards. Further, print, visual imagery, and sound (multiple modalities) are combined and juxtaposed to carry meaning.

Meanings are tied to different discourses and semiotic domains. One's literacy in Hiphop discourse, for example, is limited if one is not actively engaged in those communities of practice. Participants can potentially give deeper meanings to rap texts and performances. *Hiphop Literacies* has two particular aims. The first aim is to locate rap/Hiphop discourse, particularly, its pop culture forms, within a trajectory of Black discourses, relating them to the lived experiences of Black people, emanating from their quest for self-realization, their engagement in a discursive dialectic between various vernacular and dominant discourses and semiotic systems. Though many argue that Black popular culture, especially rap, is corporately orchestrated, and therefore a product representing debased market values, I base my argument in this book in part on commercial Hiphop/rap discourse, precisely because it is the "hardest" case. It is easier to prove that overtly socially conscious Hiphop/rap forms involve Black critical literacy/discourse, if only because they may promote stronger Afrocentric messages, more traditional formulations of Black lifestyles. This vantage point highlights how Black social actors read the world they inhabit and use available resources to struggle against forces that would annihilate them.

The second aim of this book is to examine African American Hiphop in secondary oral contexts. The primary oral practices from which Hiphop emanates are largely forged from existing African ideologies and social practices and those that the people of Black African descent encountered, developed and/or appropriated in the context of negotiating life in Anglo-dominant societies. The secondary orality comes into being in today's highly technological societies, "in which a new orality is sustained by telephone, radio, television, and other electronic devices that depend for their existence and functioning on writing and print." (Ong 1982/2002: 11) The present study considers, therefore, rap music and song lyrics, electronic and digital media, including video games, music videos, telecommunication devices, magazines, "Hiphop" novels, oral performances, and cinema. These sites are explored to uncover the distinct oral and semiotic forms that contribute to the universe of Black discourse, the influence of this diffusion of Black discourse throughout our contemporary global society. In attempting to do this work, I bring together issues and concepts that are explored in disciplines of folklore, ethnomusicology, sociolinguistics, discourse studies, and New Literacies Studies. The research extends my earlier work in *African American Literacies* (2003) and that of other scholars in the aforementioned fields.

In Chapter 1, "Black/Folk/Discoursez: OutKast and 'The Whole World,'" I theorize the development of African American Vernacular Discourses (AAVD) and locate these in genre systems within Black diasporic discourses and in selected idioms, with a brief overview of the sociocultural, historical, political, and economic contexts for the development of Afrodiasporic expressive practices. Here, I define and summarize the scope of the project. Using examples from rap performances by the phenomenal, globally known Black Southern group OutKast. In Chapter 2, "Crosscultural Vibrations: The Shared Language of Contestation of Jamaican Dancehallas and American Hiphoppas," I present an angle of analysis that links

Jamaican Dancehall discourse to African American Hiphop as variant expressions fed by common ancestors and historical and contemporary forces. Through lyrics, interviews, and review of pertinent literature, I illuminate cultural–linguistic similarities in Jamaican and African American discourses of self-definition, self-assertion, and survival in the face of globalization. The centerpiece of this chapter is an analysis of shared vocabulary and shared background. In Chapter 3, "Young Women and Critical Hiphop Literacies: Their Readings of the World," I present African American female adolescent discourse practices surrounding performances of culture, gender, and sexuality in society, as explored in the genre of the "hood novel" and in the negotiated reception of a video in the taped conversation of three African American females. This situated multimodal analysis of youth language and literacy practices focuses on tensions in stereotypical uses of language, broadly conceived, and the lived experiences of our youth. "Ride or Die B, Jezebel, Lil' Kim or Kimberly Jones and African American Women's Language and Literacy Practices: The Naked Truf," Chapter 4, focuses on the perjury trial of rapper Kimberly Jones and the United States government's subtle employment of the myth of the immoral Black Jezebel in American society to vilify her. I pay particular attention to the prosecutors' underlying language ideologies and the language and literacy traditions upon which Jones drew to combat them. My thesis is that both Jones as a Black female and Lil' Kim the Queen Bee were tried and found to be immoral liars. Chapter 5, "'Yo Mein Rap Is Phat Wie Deine Mama': African American Language in Online German Hiphop or Identifying the Global in Global Hiphop," explores the sociolinguistic consequences of the globalization of African American Language (AAL) and culture into other languages through Hiphop discourse practices, particularly as they appear in online German Hiphop. Root issues explored here are cultural globalization/localization and African American Hiphop culture, and language contact as it is reflected on the Internet. I examine the incorporation of AAL into the written online texts of German Hiphoppas, speculating on the motivation behind the use of AAL and the role of AAL/Hiphop in this context. The discussion is based on language samples gleaned from German language-based Hiphop websites, compiled and classified within frameworks that are popularly understood in sociolinguistics as codeswitching, language borrowing, or language crossing. A related analysis is offered in Chapter 6, "Hiphop and Video Games." Here I analyze the incorporation of Hiphop signs, sounds, images, and language in video games. I am interested in the social knowledge circulated in this current phase of technological imperialism—"the relationship between the ways in which . . . [Black culture is] no longer tied to locality or community, but rather operate[s] globally in conjunction with these other scapes—mediascapes, ethnoscapes, technoscapes, financescapes and ideoscapes." (Pennycook, 2003: 523)

It is my hope that my work will contribute to the growing body of scholarship that encourages educational institutions more fully to incorporate the study of literacy, particularly literacies of popular culture, more broadly into the official curriculum to stem racist social practices in society. The profession must incorporate and make widely known the work of African American and Black language and literacy scholars in order to halt the reification and reproduction of negative aspects of Eurocentric and outmoded views of learning. (Makoni *et al.*, 2003) Our students have a wealth of knowledge about the world in which they live. Our pedagogies must advance accordingly.

1

BLACK/FOLK/DISCOURSEZ

OutKast and "The Whole World"

Although rap music and Hiphop elements have been adopted and adapted by many cultures around the world,[1] this chapter, indeed this book, focuses on Hiphop discourse as a subgenre and discourse system within the universe of Black discourse which includes African American Vernacular English (AAVE) and African American Music (AAM) among other diasporic expressions. The central question that guides this analysis is: How do rappers display, on the one hand, an orientation to their situated, public role as performing products, and, on the other, that their performance is connected to discourses of authenticity and resistance? An aspect of my project is to shed light on the connection between the discursive (dis)invention of identity and the (dis)invention of language. In attempting to do this, I bring together issues and concepts that are explored in disciplines of folklore, ethnomusicology, sociolinguistics, and discourse studies. I begin by defining African American Vernacular Discourse (AAVD) as a genre system within Black diasporic discourses and in a selected sample of its various idioms, with a brief overview of the sociocultural, political, and economic contexts for selected genres. I then turn to an exploration of the function and use of Hiphop/rap discourse, using the example of a rap performance by the African American Southern rap group OutKast. The analysis is informed by principles of Critical Discourse Analysis (CDA). Discourse is central to social practices and questions of power and can benefit from CDA which foregrounds the hierarchy of social structure and social inequality, unequal power arrangements. CDA illuminates the expression of such in its examination of the multiple and contradictory nature of signs and discourses. The semiosis of symbols, signs, and visual imagery are also analyzed as part of discourse as they too reflect these social practices. (Halliday, 1978; Fairclough and Chouliaraki, 1999; Sebeok, 2001; van Dijk, 2001)

Black and African American Vernacular Discourses

The concept and practice of Black discourse refers to the collective consciousness and expression of people of Black African descent. This consciousness reflects (unconscious and conscious) ancestral and everyday knowledge. Broadly speaking, the designation the Diaspora of Black Discourse(s) allows us to group a range of

1

African, Neo-African, and Afro-American language varieties, expressive forms, and linguistic ideologies for comparative analysis of specific historical, political, socio-cultural, and sociolinguistic features. Via slavery, colonization, neo-imperialism, migration, wars, global technological processes, and diasporic crossing, Continental Africans and their descendants participate in the (dis)invention and global flow of Black discourse. Black discourses are a direct result of African–European contact on the shores of West Africa and in what became the New World. For example, the use of English by Africans originated for purposes of negotiation and trade, initiated by Europeans. In 1554, the Englishman William Towerson took five Africans from a British territory in West Africa known as the Gold Coast to England, to learn English, to become interpreters. Three of these Africans returned to the Gold Coast in 1557. Thus, 1557 is accepted as the beginning of the African use of English (Dalby, 1970). We could say that Africans were already at a dis-advantage because they were in the position of learning a language of trade and commerce while having no familiarity with its total system. In a language learning situation like this one, critical and multiple consciousnesses are built into the language acquisition process. In other words, a group makes the new language fit, to the extent possible, its epistemological, ontological, and cosmological system. This is how we can say that there are uniquely Black versions of English, French, Dutch, and Portuguese, for which Robert Williams and his associates coined "Ebonics." Other scholars, Africologists, consider all forms of Ebonics as new African languages, rather than Black versions of European languages.[2] Rickford and Rickford (2000) offer a balanced explanation, pointing out African, European, and creole sources for various language patterns in US Ebonics, for example. Most scholars of language agree that when Africans and Europeans "met," their lan-guages mingled to create new African- and European-influenced language systems. One thing is for sure, people of African descent have evolved and contributed Ebonic and Pan African discourses to the world wherever they have found them-selves on the continent and in the diaspora, bringing with them that flava and spirit of survival. Dalby (1970: 4) gives a useful outline of this phenomenon:

> "Black" enables us to group together a wide range of speech forms, on both sides of the Atlantic, in which a largely European vocabulary is coupled with grammatical and phonological features reminiscent of West African languages: . . . The clearest examples of ["Black Atlantic"] languages are what may be termed "creoles" or "creolized languages," in each of which the divergence from the original European language has been so great that one may consider a new language to have come into being, no longer inter-intelligible with its European counterpart.

> Examples of these creole languages are found on both sides of the Atlantic, especially in the Caribbean and along the West African coast. At the other end of the scale of Black Atlantic languages are the dialectal variants of European languges which, although directly identifiable with Black speakers, have remained largely intelligible to White speakers of the

same languages, [African] American English and Jamaican English (as opposed to Jamaican creole) may be cited as examples, in which the structural influence of West African languages—although very much reduced—may nevertheless be clearly traced.[3]

Although it is often helpful to understand language from a structural-grammatical perspective, this view of language can obscure the fact that it is history, culture, and lived experience. As stated by Brathwaite (1993: 266) in his discussion of the "History of the Voice": "It may be in English [for example], but often it is in an English which is like a howl, or a shout, or a machine-gun, or the wind, or a wave. It is also like the Blues. And sometimes it is English and African at the same time." This is why I am so interested in Black language as discourse. Black discourses are not fixed and static. They are dynamic and reflexive systems of "behaving, inter-acting, valuing, thinking, believing, speaking, and often reading and writing that are accepted as instantiations of particular roles . . . by specific groups of . . . people . . . [Black] Discourses are ways of being ['an African descendant']. They are 'ways of being in the world'; they are 'forms of life'. They are, thus, always and every-where *social* and products of social histories." (Adapted from Gee, 1996: viii) It is

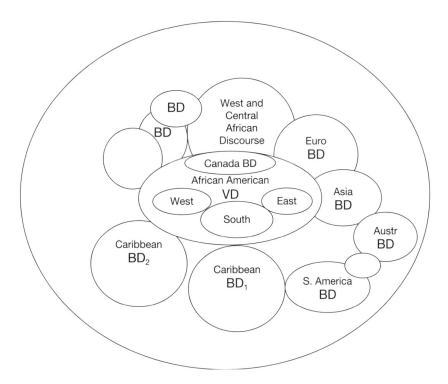

Figure 1.1 Diaspora(s) of Black discourse

important to draw attention to the inclusion of reading and writing or Africanized literacy in the definition of Black discourse, as literacy is informed by discourse and is an ideologically charged social construction. (Richardson, 2003)

In the North American context, we can identify AAVDs by manifestations of their many signature themes and forms. They include the various sociocultural forms and institutions developed by African Americans to express their distinctive existence. From this perspective, there are African American ways of being and communicating that derive from particular histories, geographies, and social locations. Some of these ways of being were developed during slavery and influenced by two crucial factors: the demand from dominant Whites that all manner of behavior and communication of African people display their compliance with domination and supposed inferiority; and African people's resistance to this demand "through the use of existing African [communication] systems of indirectness." (Morgan, 2002: 24) As Morgan explains, "indirectness includes an analysis of discourses of power . . . Once the phenomenology of indirectness operated both within white supremacist encounters and African American culture and social encounters, interactions, words or phrases could have contradictory or multiple meanings beyond traditional English interpretations." The grammatical and pronunciation patterns of AAVE are often analyzed as apart from its ideological-discursive aspects for purposes of structural analysis. In this project, the emphasis is on AAVE and AAM as part and parcel of AAVD, as all of these are inextricably linked systems and are a direct result of African–European contact on the shores of West Africa and in what became the New World. In the present work, AAVE includes the broad repertoire of themes and cultural practices as well as narrowly conceived verbal surface features used by many historic and contemporary African Americans, which indicate an alternate worldview. In other words, AAVE represents the totality of vernacular expression. AAVE should be understood as African American survival culture. On the level of language, although the majority of the words are English in origin, their meanings are historically and contextually situated relevant to the experiences of African Americans. Further, a point that is often overlooked is that there is a Standard AAVE. Scholars of AAVE argue for an expanded conception of it, whereby many speakers command a wide range of forms on the continuum from more creole-like to more standardized forms. In this sense, "an educated, middle-class [B]lack person may express his or her identification with African American culture, free of the stigma attached to nonstandard speech [/grammar]" (DeBose, 1992: 159)[4]

To put it another way, African American Standard and Vernacular discourses are in dialectical relation and are in dialogic relation to other diasporic discourses, American discourses, as well as other global discourses. By extending the definition of African American language usage beyond (surface level) syntax, phonology, and vocabulary, etc. into (deep-level) speech acts, nonverbal behavior, and cultural production, the role of language as a major influence in reality construction and symbolic action is emphasized. The multiethnicity of symbols is more apparent in this view.[5]

1557	1619	1661	1808	1863	1877	1914–45	1966	1990s
Beginning of African use of English	20 African slaves/indentured servants arrive at Jamestown on a Dutch ship	Beginning of slave codes circumscribing activities and lives of slaves	Outlawing of Slave Trade; rise of Anti-Slavery Movement	Emancipation	Reconstruction ends; institutionalization of "separate but equal"	World Wars I and II; vast urban migration of Blacks out of South	Black Power Movement; push for integration comes to a halt	Capitalist, post-industrialist crises creating severe problems for some Blacks; unparalleled prosperity for others
Pidgin		**Creole**	**De-creolization De-Africanization**			De-creolization continues	**Re-creolization Re-Africanization**	
					De-creolized forms solidify, especially among underclass/"field" slave descendants		De-creolization halted; conscious attempt to recapture earlier Black Language forms and create new ones	Emergence of bilingual consciousness; linguistic experimentation
	African		**Colored**			**Negro**	**Black**	**African American**

Figure 1.2 Smitherman's model of U.S. Ebonics and the Black experience

Everyday experiences of African Americans require heightened attention to language use and ritual performance. Uniquely Black usages of language occur in most domains of life, including Street Life, Church Life, Politics and others. Thus, theorizing about African American language use requires emphasis on rhetorical context, the language users, their history, values, sociocultural, political, and economic position. (Debose, 2001) Smitherman's model of U.S. Ebonics and the Black Experience (1987/2000: 36) is helpful in visualizing, for example, the complex context that shapes African Americans' use of language in the New World and what became the United States from 1557 through the 1990s.

Not only does Smitherman's model allow for the linguistic continuum concept, wherein speakers can potentially move up or down different linguistic zones, one end of which is closer to a European language/culture and the other of which is comprised of a creole form characterized by more African-derived features (Alleyne, 1980; Rickford, 1987), her model also emphasizes the social world which influences how language is interpreted, defined, conceived, performed, with other expressions and symbols and juxtaposed against such to (re)interpret reality. One must be mindful that the horizontal or vertical conceptualization of the continuum can subordinate the heteroglossic and layered nature of discourse. In other words, the linguistic continuum cannot be separated from the sociocultural continuum. From the enslavement era through the present, African American beliefs and practices are informed by those of various African cultures and respond to, borrow from, and negotiate the practices of the dominant culture. The social locations of the performer and the audience determine how meaning is interpreted. Social actors can manipulate certain elements within the continuum in line with their rhetorical goals. When we think of African American language as inseparable from African American discourse, we keep in mind the cultural frames, performance traditions, idioms, etc. that inform the expressive forms, the senses and sounds of real people conveying meaning to each other within the context of a shared (or not, depending on one's social location) set of assumptions about the nature of the world. Portia Maultsby's (1991: 186) representation of the development of African American music is helpful.

Residing on the uppermost part of the Black Diaspora discourse continua are diverse West and Central African beliefs and practices/West and Central African Communication Patterns/and West and Central African Musical Roots. In general, across each of these domains respectively, we can identify an African ethos that extended to the so-called New World context, beginning in the seventeenth century, encompassing both sacred and secular speech, expressions, and musical idioms. Though Smitherman (2000: 1) is focusing on American Black Talk, her sentiments relate on the level of the African Diaspora. She writes: "Black Talk crosses boundaries of age, gender, region, religion, and social class because it all comes from the same source: the [Black] Experience and the [African] oral tradition embedded in that experience."

In the enslavement era in the North American context, the speech was more creole-like; the work songs employed African-oriented vocal shadings and

AFRICAN AMERICAN MUSIC: ITS DEVELOPMENT

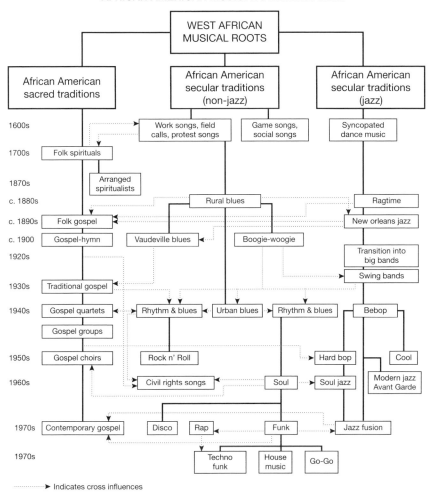

Figure 1.3 Maultsby's model: African American music: its development

polyrhythm to transform everyday experience into sound; the field hollers imitated sounds in the natural environment; folktales invoked African values, proverbs, and characters; protest songs included Africanized indirection, signifying, and critique; the spirituals employed African-derived melodies, harmonics, call and response, and promoted African-influenced understandings of spirit possession.

Let me, briefly, give two historical examples of the African performance tradition: corn shucking and juba. In one sense, the performances involved in corn shucking helped the enslaved to organize and endure the work of harvest time. They used songs and games to make the work bearable. The lyrics and the sound

7

creation fed their inner and outer needs for spiritual and self-upliftment. Inwardly, the music, through its use of call–response and improvisation, provided an individual and communal soul-liberating experience. Outwardly, the occasion of the corn shucking and its accompanying festivity was an opportunity for the enslaved to be served by the house servants or sometimes even Ole Missus and Master, and to comment lyrically on life as they saw it. The lyrics below demonstrate such commentary:

> Shuck corn, shell corn,
> Carry corn to mill.
> Grind de meal, gimme de husk;
> Bake de bread, gimme de crus';
> Fry de meat, gimme de skin';
> And dat's de way to bring 'em in.
> (Perrow, 1915: 139)

I believe the verbal art of "shuckin' and jivin'" evolved from this survival strategy of performing the corn shucking during the 1800s. Clarence Major (1970/1994) defines shuckin' and jivin' as "originally, southern 'Negro' expression for clowning, lying, pretense," with the term originating around the 1870s.

Similarly, juba—the eating of unwanted food—was sung, danced, and patted out polyrhythmically to endure the harsh conditions under which these people labored. As explained by Beverly Robinson (1990: 216), "To prepare psychologically to eat what was usually labeled slop, [the enslaved people] made up a song that sounded like merriment but carried a double message." Plantation owners would invite their friends over to have the song performed for them for their enjoyment. The owners were never aware of the meanings signified through the song as seen in a brief excerpt recalled by Bessie Jones below, comprising lyrics side by side with a translation:

Juba this and Juba that	Means giblet this [a little of this] and /Giblet that [a little of that]
Juba killed a yella' cat	Because they couldn't say mixed-up Food might kill the white folks. They was afraid to say that because white folks'd kill them.

Stereotyping is a dynamic phenomenon, historically shaped by the actions of both enslavers, who sought to control the enslaved, and by the enslaved to thwart the imposition. During the early nineteenth century, White blackface minstrelsy became the most popular form of entertainment. This phenomenon had the further effect of "divest[ing] [B]lack people of control over elements of their culture and over their own cultural representation generally." (Lott, 1996: 6) Ironically, by the

8

end of the nineteenth century, the only performance opportunities open to Black performers were via minstrel houses, where they had to compete with the counterfeit representations of blackness provided by the White minstrels. The minstrel example provides us with a microcosmic look at the tensions embedded within discourse in society. Discourses are affected by societal phenomena and represent competing worldviews. This is not to suggest that the foundation of Black discourse is opposition to White discourse. As Smitherman (1977/1986: 42) explains, "many aspects of black . . . behavior are Africanized adaptations which can be seen as logical cultural consequences rather than as strictly racially based [sociocultural forms] reflecting black reactions to whiteness." Thus, in our analyses of each era and domain of the African American experience, we must bring to bear the contexts that influence African American expression. To put it crudely: Slavery/ rural–agrarian, Reconstruction/rural–sharecropping, Harlem Renaissance/ rural–urban–industrial, Civil Rights/Black Power/post-industrial, and now Post-Civil Rights/informational, global digital, and technological/service oriented.

In this age of global information and digitization of knowledge, those with the means of global distribution control dominant definitions and representations of certain discourses through commerce. This is also true from an historical perspective. Black cultural producers had no control over outside interpretation of their work.

A working definition of African American rap/Hiphop discourse

Why study Hiphop discourse? Hiphop is a rich site of cultural production that has pervaded and been pervaded by almost every American institution and has made an extensive global impact. Hiphop discourse, no matter how commodified or "blaxploited," offers an interesting view of the human freedom struggle and aspects of the knowledge that people have about the world. As discussed most eloquently by Houston Baker (1984) in *Blues, Ideology, and Afro-American Literature: A Vernacular Theory*, all Afro American narrative can be traced (in part) to an "economics of slavery" and is tied to a bill of sale. Thus, like "traditional" African American language data, Hiphop discourse tells us a lot about socioeconomic stratification and the struggle between culture and capital. Hiphop discourse, like previous Afro-American expressive forms, is a Black creative response to absence and desire and a site of epistemological development. Though it is often seen as mere corporate orchestration, Hiphop is a site of identity negotiation. Unlike "traditional" African American language data, commercial Hiphop discourse is wholly centered within the new capitalism. The aspect of the new capitalism that pertains to this study is "knowledge work." That is, the insider's knowledge that business and industry uses to design products to tap certain values and create consumer identities by manipulating symbols and markets. This knowledge is recontextualized and recycled in the space of commercial Hiphop performances promoting stereotypical "commonsense" ideas about African Americans and deflects attention away from

9

the poor social conditions that make certain occupations or preoccupations a welcome means of survival. As such Hiphop is both associated with ethnic (Black) and national (general American) consciousness.

This being the case, many would argue that there is no authentic culture to study in rap music or Hiphop discourse for mass consumption, since rap has long become a global industry removed from its primary audience. However, study of folk culture is not constrained to isolated groups untouched by contemporary postindustrial society. Folk are "the people who know," who have a special knowledge from their vantage point of the world, from their routine social experiences. The discourses in which they participate are always already hybrid. From this perspective, any group can be a folk group. The study of folk groups in the contemporary world involves studying their hybridity, an aspect of which can be examined through studying the impact of technologies on the interaction of discourses between audience, performer, and the making of meaning. (Kelley, 1992)

Hiphop discourse is a genre system of AAVE/Black discourse. I prefer AAVE to encompass the other genres within the African American discourse communities because in relation to dominant discourse the total genre system is vernacular or counterlinguistic. I want to emphasize here that this counter-reality is reflective of constant engagement with dominant notions of reality. As a starting point, we may see Hiphop discourse as a subsystem in relation to African American and other discourses, as in Figure 1.4.

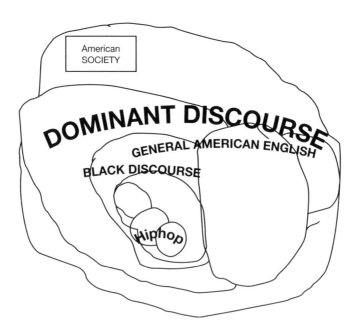

Figure 1.4 Hiphop as a subsystem within African American discourse and its relation to other discourses

Hiphop language can be defined as influenced by African oral traditions of rhythmic "'talk-singing [signifying], blending reality and fiction,' and [in the mainstream] it has come to mean any kind of strong talk or rap." (Smitherman, 1994: 190) Additional African language practices employed in rap lyrics are call–response, tonal semantics, semantic inversion/flippin the script, mimicry, narrativizing, toasting, boasting/braggadocio, image-making, and punning.

Call–response is used to draw the listener into the performance. A performer uses some lyrical hook or refrain that can be easily repeated by the listener. For example, an emcee (preferred term for a skilled lyricist) shouts, "Where the real Hiphop at?" The proper response from engaged participants is: "Over here," thus showing participation. Tonal semantics refers to the use of vocal inflection and vocal rhythm to convey meaning. Semantic inversion or flippin the script refers to turning a meaning into its opposite or divesting a concept of its received meaning to inscribe one reflective of the speaker's experience. Mimicry, the imitation of sounds, has the effect of critique in many cases and is used in signifying, which refers to the employment of indirection to make a point or to poke fun. Narrativizing is the storytelling mode consisting of reliving and dramatization of what went on or what is imagined to happen in the future. Toasting refers to folk poetics, while boasting and braggadocio are narrative traditions wherein the speaker/rapper asserts his or her superb and many times exaggerated characteristics or abilities. Image-making is the use of metaphorical language, tending toward the graphic, the concrete, and, for its effect, punning depends on witty use of signifiers/terms with multiple referents. (See Smitherman, 1977/1986, for fuller definitions with extended examples; see also Smitherman, 2000, for a discussion of the "Communicative Practices of the Hiphop nation.")

Hiphop language has an obvious attitude. It is graphic "and it adheres to the pronunciation and grammar of [AAVE]." (Smitherman, 1994: 18) The Hiphop lexicon is largely provided by AAVE speakers, with some words donated from Spanish, Caribbean Englishes, and from graffiti vocabulary (argot). "Hiphop's language ideology is consciously and often defiantly based on urban African American norms, values, and popular culture constructed against dominant cultural and linguistic norms. It thus relies on the study, knowledge, and use of [AAVE] and General American Vernacular English [GAVE] linguistic features and principles of grammaticalization." (Morgan, 2001: 188) As such, AAVE discourses, in any of their genres, are highly reflexive systems of communication. By reflexive I mean that certain linguistic/semiotic/discourse/literacy practices are used in certain contexts precisely because of the situation of use. Historically, African American language and people have been represented in society as coming from a debased culture, and that's the best-case scenario. The worse is that Blacks have no culture, no language. This rhetorical situation should draw attention to the ways in which Hiphop discourse, like other Black discourse, is masked inside English as lingua franca. Black discourses are survival francas, since their use is tied to capital, which one needs to survive in this world. The notion of linguistic market seems particularly appropriate here: "The linguistic market, in fact, is part of a broader symbolic market, and one can see the self as the commodity that is being produced for value in the market. Thus one is both agent and commodity." (Eckert, 2000: 13) From this vantage point, the sounds, visual images, identities, labels, names, etc. associated with Afro American language, discourses, and people are largely a heterogeneous set established historically, institutionally, and economically by those with power to assign meaning, worth, and value.

This presents a dilemma for rap performers, since their narratives are commodified in the global economy of rap music and Hiphop culture, leaving them in the popular imagination as agentless narrators compliant in their own oppression. The mantra of Hiphoppas, "keep it real," reflects their preoccupation with authenticity, which is often popularly understood as emphasis on surviving in a hostile society, variously interpreted as the hood, the streets, the system, "the real." The ability to survive, "to make a way outta no way," and to narrate this experience rhythmically in such a way that it resonates with the primary audience, is what is at stake in evaluation of rappers' performance, delivery, style, as authentic. Given that rap music and rappers are seen as commodities globally marketed largely by exploitation of stereotypical language and images of "niggas," "pimps," "gangstas," "militants," "hos," "bitches," and "bucks," how do they display, on the one hand, an orientation to their situated, public role as performing products, and, on the other, that their performance is connected to discourses of authenticity and resistance? This study takes up these aspects of communication together with the social, cultural, and political positioning of social actors. In the few examples I discuss here, I focus on the relationship between linguistic and social stereotypes. These stereotypes are realized on the levels of both surface features and discourse. I employ the term stereotype in two senses. In the first, it is used to refer to a generic cultural model, the way that we understand and organize the world, storylines, connected images, informal theories, received symbolic forms, "shared by people belonging to specific social or cultural groups." (Gee, 1999: 81) In the second it refers to dominant discourse practices concerning African Americans, including "commonsense" prejudiced statements and discriminatory behavior that often go uncontested as normal and acceptable. What I hope to demonstrate is rappers' exploitation of linguistic stereotypes to upset and redefine social reality from meanings rooted in their everyday experiences, thereby (dis)inventing identity and language. In what follows, I will offer examples of rappers' (dis)invention of dominant and socially constructed stereotypes.

"OutKast" of the whole world

To reiterate, the communicative styles and ways of knowing of the performers can be traced to Black vernacular expressive arts developed by African Americans as resistance and survival strategies. Many of the experiences, such as racism, police brutality, miseducation, and identity imposition, are issues which are fundamental to the African American struggle and are dealt with in various cultural expressions. Thus, rap performances, like all expressive forms, must be considered in relation to beliefs, values, mores, and complex ideologies that underlie the street apparel, hard body imagery, and the sometimes seeming celebration of misogyny, thuggishness, and larger-than-life personas narrated in the music. One way to look at the celebration of gangsta practices, thuggishness, rampant materialism, and seeming disrespect for law and mainstream values in Hiphop is in relation to Black vernacular folk epic story and song tradition.

In African American culture, there are two character types in particular that appear in rap music—the "bad nigger" and the badman or badwoman. The "bad nigger" is a type of trickster who defies dominant mainstream values and sometimes those of traditional Afro-American culture. He "threatens the solidarity and harmony of the group" and may bring potential harm to everyone. (Roberts, 1989: 199) Conversely, the badman/badwoman is an amalgamation of the trickster and the conjurer and is associated with a secular lifestyle that appeals to some segments of the Black community, for badmanism offered an alternate route to success through gambling or some other illegal activities. (Roberts, 1989: 206) The badman often resorted to gun violence in an act of self-defense or victimization. Imani Perry's (2004: 107) discussion of the outlaw aesthetic in Afro American culture is very instructive:

> The outlaw image appears in very obvious symbols and metaphors in the music, but it also exists on a more esoteric level in the intellectual world of hip hop. The name of the rap duo OutKast is brilliant for its concise articulation and celebration of the life behind the Du Boisian veil. The ease with which African Americans can accept conspiracy theories as truth lends evidence to this distinct outcast epistemological framework. Given the inconsistency between the constitutional and symbolic meanings of Americanness and the experiences of African Americans, we are left with a healthy suspicion and curiosity. OutKast centralizes the position of Otherness as a site of privileged knowledge and potential.

The performance embodied in the recording and video of the song "The Whole World" by the rap duo OutKast seems highly reflexive and explicitly conscious of the rhetorical situation. It employs several contentious stereotypes and is careful to connect itself to the blues and jazz traditions. The performance isn't easily dismissed as wholesale corporate orchestration. The music, lyrics, and visuals invoke meanings through sounds, images, and ideographs that underscore the discursive dialectic of dominant and vernacular discourses.

In the examples that follow, it is helpful to keep in mind that stereotypes associated with the South also affected rappers who were seen as "country" and backward until "Dirty South" rap caught on. Although we can cite numerous Southern rap songs that invoke angst, aggression, and opposition to the status quo, Southern rap can still be identified by some industry powerbrokers as happy music.[6] Rapper David Banner explains, "Many labels look at Southern rap as happy black music because there is so much emotion in it. But because we're not time-traveling through the pyramids doesn't mean we can't be deep."[7]

13

Figure 1.5 Representation of rapper in clownish white face/voodoo-styled makeup by Sara-Eve Rivera

"The Whole World" video is set in the Big Top, the circus. Both the setting and the title suggest a major theme of the song: the whole world is a stage, life is a play, and everyone is cast in supporting roles. Though the lead actors are expected to bring their own knowledge of the world into their characters, the roles are scripted. One has to be very creative to manipulate meaning inside this structure. The circus decontextualizes and exploits performances by trained animals, people, or clowns, for example, and (re)presents them as strange, spectacular, or exotic. Similarly, the apparatuses of the global world power reduce culture to decontextualized commodities and cultural workers to panderers. These themes are demonstrated throughout the performance. One of the rappers, Andre, is wearing white face, clownish, voodoo-styled makeup and a blond wig, which invokes a host of associations.

In its popular digital representation, the painted Black male is presented as spectacle, invoking, as his makeup suggests, a clownish–voodooish image. The Black man as clown reinscribes the mocking image of a "backward" people—not

14

to be taken seriously. But upon further inspection we know that the clown's surface movements and expressions of hilarity reflect solemn observations about the human condition. Similarly, voodoo as a cultural practice and way of understanding the world became taboo among most Americans and reduced to a commodity, thriving in dominant discourse as witchcraft, fortune-telling, "mumbo-jumbo." In the popular imagination voodoo is cheap entertainment, something that can be bought for $1.99 per minute from actors like "Miss Cleo." In the North American South, voodoo was a total belief system that included ancestral religious traditions as well as herbal and medical care for the oppressed community unavailable to them by any other means.

Concomitantly, the Black male wearing white face image troubles the central concepts of minstrelsy: the presentation of authentic blackness by Whites, alternatively termed the White stereotype of blackness; and the White stereotype of whiteness. The white paint and the blond wig on a Black body symbolize Whites' view of blackness through whiteness, and Blacks' distortion of "superior" whiteness. Conversely, Blacks' struggle against this imposed worldview creates authenticity within Black culture.

Not only do visual images in the video represent these contesting discourses; AAVE phonological and lexical systems are also employed by the rappers to (dis)invent or reinscribe and upset stereotypes, such as that of the Ignorant N_____. Historically, racist discourse imbued the Southern Black person (and lower-class Whites) with qualities such as "slow", "dimwitted".[8] Their speech supposedly reflected their limitations. However, many African American speech patterns are remnants of African heritage, or reinterpretations of English. In either case, they are part of African American culture. Conscious use of such speech patterns then on the part of African American rappers signals their refusal of a negative evaluation of their Black heritage.

The Black speech pattern vocalized intersyllabic /r/ is used in the first lyrical phrase of the song: "Yeah I'm afraid like I'm sca'ed as a dog." Conscious inscription of Black Southern identity linguistically ushers forth both Black and dominant interpretations of the meaning of this phrase. This pattern of employing Southern Black speech is continued throughout and realized in the rapper's use of lexical items such as "sing" and "along" as [saNg] and [ŭlooNg], where the medial vowel sound, the open o, is prolonged to produce a stereotypical "Southern drawl." This elongated open o occurs four times in the opening verse of the song. Inventing and then rupturing the symbols of Black Southern ignorance underscores the synthetic nature of language.

AAVE verbs such as "git down" (In the line "the whole worl loves it when you don't git down, ohwn") are employed in a way that defies unequivocal interpretation. "Git down" means "to do something enthusiastically" or to make progress. However, in this context it is preceded by the negator "don't." As such, the phrase could mean "don't git up," the opposite of "git down" (or to make no progress). This coupled with the AAVE phonological marker [ɪ] in "git" where more mainstream varieties of English use [ɛ] invokes multiple and competing

15

discourses. In this sense, "don't git down" is an example of signifying, where signifying is "a way of encoding messages or meanings which involves, in most cases, an element of indirection" (Mitchell-Kernan quoted in Gates, 1988: 80). A mainstream American English interpretation of "don't git down" is "don't feel sad." Historically, this stereotype invokes the happy darky. Recall that Black sociocultural forms such as juba were interpreted by outsiders to represent the enslaved populations' contentment with their condition as represented by their singing and dancing. This interpretation becomes more apparent when examined within the context of the chorus, where the phrase occurs, which I take to represent the thematic significance of the song. The chorus phrase "Cause the whole worl loves it when you don't git down" is functioning as a cohesive device. The chorus begins with the discourse connector "Cause." This suggests support or evidence for the views expressed in the lines that precede it. One reading of the phrase is: the whole world knows about Blacks, in this case the stereotype presented, the Ignorant N/Ignorant Southern N.

Another discourse marker used to (re)invent or (re)present and contest the Ignorant N stereotype is onomatopoeia, as it is used to represent non-sense syllables, though of course they make sense to the utterer. In recurring lines of the chorus, the onomatopoeic phrase, sung in a jazz-scat style, "Bah bah da, bah bah bah da da," symbolizes dissonance between dominant and Black culture and their differences in the consumption of Black sociocultural forms. Onomatopoeia is a sign whose phonetic shape resembles its referent in some sense. In this context, then, the non-sense syllables are representative of the decontextualized and digitally diffused Black sound. For the primary audience, ultimately, Black sounds function to sustain life, but as we move away from the primary rap audience, or from the origins of Black culture, Black sounds are not fully understood as core culture but appreciated as popular sources of revenue, entertainment, and Black Noise.

Metaphorical variation also indexes the Ignorant N/Southern Black identity stereotype. The phrase "Yeah I'm afraid like I'm sca'ed as a dog," already mentioned, invokes the stereotype of the unreasonably afraid unmanly subhuman coward which was made popular at the height of White American minstrelsy. Similarly, another metaphor employed in the lyrics, "raining inside" (as in "this is the way that we walk on a sunny day when it's raining inside and you're all alooown"), signifies a dark and dreary existence or a blues mood. As I've already indicated, the metaphor "don't git down" invokes the "happy darky."

The next example employs metaphorical variation and /r/variation, signaled in zero postvocalic r, as in the following: "Whateva floats yo boat or finds yo los remote." The interpretations of the metaphor "whateva floats yo boat" in the context of this performance signal floating as the ability to go with the tide, "life preservance," "being suspended near the surface," and "fluctuating freely in relationship to other currencies, as determined by supply and demand: said of a currency" (*Webster's New World College Dictionary*). Certainly these possible meanings implicate the commodification of Black performance but they also raise the issue of a certain agency within that commodification. Similarly, "Finds yo los remote" indicates movement away in time or in space as a method of agency. Taken together, the metaphors in these lines point to the continuity of the struggle, whether survival strategies are interpreted as superficial and contemporary or distant and historical, they are deeply rooted, interconnected, and linked to the interlocking systems of racism, patriarchy, and capitalism.

The stereotype of the Bad N_____ is invoked, inscribed, and upset by several African American communication practices, among them /r/vocalization, the dozens, braggadocio, and homonymy. Most of the uses of intersyllabic and post-vocalic /r/occur in words or phrases which signal the badman language tradition in Afro American folklore. The badman's roots are in the African trickster. In the North American context, he surfaces in animal tales. As previously mentioned, the badman also represents defiance of White authority from slavery through freedom:

> He is disdainful of social conventions . . . breaks rules, violates taboos, and
> . . . is not intimidated by the law, the police, or even the devil . . . Despite
> the fact that his exploits are self-serving and sometimes at the expense of
> his community members, (including African American women, who are
> often sexually objectified), this figure continues to endure, some folklorists
> conjecture, because he suggests a defiance to racial oppression and
> submission.
>
> (Gilyard and Wardi, 2004: 333)

For intersyllabic /r/vocalization in AAVE lexicon, we have a number of terms: "quarter" [kwatə], "shorts" [shawtz], and "sports" [spawtz]. Postvocalic /r/can be noted in terms like [heDə] "hater", [suckə] "sucker," "quarter" [kwatə], [dawtə] "daughter," "nigga" [niggə], "meter" [mItə], "neither" [nIðə], [wɛðə] "weather," [bruðə] "brother," [sɛvə] "sever,' [wutɛvə] "whatever," and [yo] "your." The commanding phrase—"Take a little trip hata pack up your mind," where "hater," the Hiphop lexical item, is a shortened version of "player hater"—indicates an envious person, one who expresses extreme dislike for another's success in any life endeavor, especially envious of one who has multiple relationships. It is also used in response to negative criticism. The persona in this verse could be understood as speaking to an oppositional audience, perhaps one which does not like or understand the rapper's performance. One of the song's lines—"I caught a sucka dyin cause he thought he could rhyme"—employs "sucka," a general AAVE term for an unhip person; it can be interpreted here as a dis, an example of signifying in the sense of witty putdown. (Smitherman 1977/1986)

The zero r in the phrases "th'ow the Porsche at you" and "th'ow a shell in it" evince AAVE badman braggadocio, and allude to Black struggle. Both literally and figuratively, the Black social actor manipulates words, materials, and identities to survive rhetorically and physically: "Th'ow the Porsche at you" refers to ways in which Black sociocultural forms serve to colonize new markets and yet offer some semblance of freedom to cultural workers. In particular, the phrase points to the rappers as sellers of American and global products and representatives of the

Table 1.1 Linguistic and social stereotypes

Variation	Semantic marker	Stereotypes	
Dominant/ Black discourse		Ignorant Nigga	Bad Nigga
Phonological	Onomatopoeia=bah bah da . . . /ang/ for /ing/ Elongated open o Vocalized intersyllabic /r/	sca'ed	qwata, spo'ts shawts (sho'ts)
	Zero postvocalic /r/		Hata, sucka qwata, dawta meta, neitha weatha, brutha seva, whuteva yo
	Zero /r/ after consonant		th'ow
Lexical	homonymy		meta/meeta breeva/breeva stage/stage battle/battle crack/crack shell/shell shades/shades
	desyllabification cultural icons/ideographs		a breeva ation cool, curl dread, nappy shell
	Hiphop words		hata (hater), rhyme battle
Metaphorical	Figurative language	sca'ed as a dog rainin inside don't git down	don't take no shawts I gotta meter (meet her) Like havin hair wit stylin gel in it Whateva floats yo boat finds ya los remote
Communication style	narrativizing signifyin	don't git down	sucka a breeva ation
	dozens braggadocio		

18

so-called American Dream. The rapper is used as a tool of oppression yet symbolizes freedom to those similarly situated in the global ranks of the dispossessed.

Homonymy is another process whereby Hiphop discourse wreaks lexical havoc against the establishment. In the lyrics of this song, several referents function as homonyms. In its technical sense, a word would have to appear more than once and be used to indicate different referents in order to be classified as a homonym. Here, however, certain words are used only once, creating a black hole, if you will, in the sense of highly condensed energy that packs multiple meanings into one signifier. The signifiers "stage" and "battle" in the context of this song could be read as underscoring the topos of role playing in the historical Black struggle, as "stage" refers multiply to "stage" as platform, "stage" as movement in time, "stage" as to represent or present. "Battle" can also be interpreted multiply as "verbal duel" or "struggle/conflict." Similarly, the term "crack" is invoked. The foremost stereotypic role that it invokes is Blacks as drug-dealers of crack cocaine. "Crack" also refers to violence as in "a sharp resounding blow." Dominant discourse has encoded the negative aspects of these stereotypes into the language and foisted them more heavily onto Blacks than other social groups. Cleverly, as he is wont to do, the rapper seeks to break this chain with his own "crack," as in "a witty remark," with language, as another pertinent sense of "crack" reveals. "Shell," referred to in the phrase "th'ow a shell in it," also functions as a homonym. It has four relevant and distinct meanings. First, it conjures a symbol of ancient Africa, the cowry shell, which has been used as money, jewelry, and as a charm, among other things. The second meaning—outside covering—refers to the "masks" that people are required to wear for various rhetorical purposes. Another possible meaning is "inside covering"—not letting the world know one's true identity or feelings. And still another is "explosive." All of these senses of "shell" draw attention to the topos of the performance of identities.

Finally, "shades" also functions homonymically. In the phrase "I take my shades off," "shades" reinforces the topic of identity performance, as "shade" indicates "darkness," "gradation of color," "difference of variation." "Shades" also references the Black way of being known as cool, since sunglasses or shades are a symbol of cool. As such, *taking one's shades off* indexes that burdensome social practice of multiplying oneself, but also the yearning toward a more unified self or unmasked self. To reiterate, these surface features represent stereotypes that are connected to discourses.

Figure 1.6 is an attempt to represent graphically the multiplicity of meanings and their reception in a crossover context—that is, who one is in relation to the performer determines the meanings that will be selected as authentic. The job of the Black performer is to manipulate and (dis)invent Black discourses as is rhetorically convenient, to open the semantic field so that there is a wider space for meaning-making potential, while simultaneously indicating privileged Black meanings that resonate within specific contexts of production and reception.

The use of stereotypes confirms an awareness of self-representation among the performers, how Black people are represented to themselves within society.

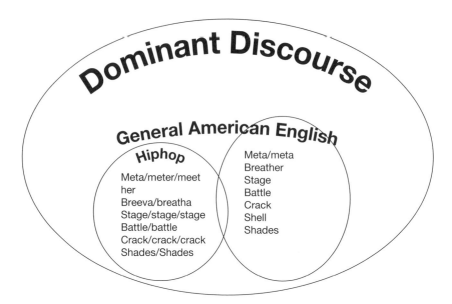

Figure 1.6 Model viewing a primary Hiphop discourse group and a non-primary audience

Rappers constantly re-create, reshape, and reinvent these forms to reaffirm Black humanity. What is often overlooked and perhaps should be restated here is that Black discourse is reflexive and reflective of the context from which it emanates: tied to capital, tied to a bill of sale, but also struggling to define self. This is true of Hiphop as a subgenre within Black discourse as well.

Figure 1.7 attempts to show how societal values are embedded within Hiphop, as Black discourses struggle for self-definition in the face and space of languages and systems of domination that would annihilate them. Although Hiphop reinvents and recycles African diasporic performance traditions and ways of knowing, it is naive to think that Black people have "somehow lived in American society for hundreds of years and yet have remained untouched, uninfluenced by the world around us. It is this romanticized notion of our blackness (the myth of the noble savage) that allows many people to refuse to see that the social orders of black [discourses are themselves stratified to the core]." (Adapted from hooks, 1981: 116) Paying serious attention to these forms may help us to understand cultural change in this current phase of global imperialism.

OutKast's performance in "The Whole World" is rich and clearly not exhausted in this brief explication. However, my point is to show that the best rap performances reflect the tensions apparent between dominant and subordinate discourses. In the tradition of Black discourse, Black social actors reject imposed definitions and seek to reinscribe their own versions of reality from their perspectives. In using these trickster discourses to survive hostile conditions, rappers exploit linguistic stereotypes to upset and redefine social reality from meanings rooted in their

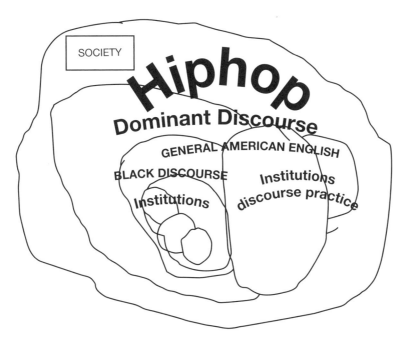

Figure 1.7 Model viewing society embedded within Hiphop

everyday experience, thereby (dis)inventing relationships between identity and language. Where conventional Anglo-American discourses attempt to ascribe certain language forms to certain identities, or particular identities to language forms, Hiphop discourses cross African American, General American English, Caribbean English, and Spanish, among other language backgrounds, to move the crowds and shift the framing of identities tied to those languages. Through African American oral traditions, they recall African language histories from before the European invention of languages and imposition of metadiscursive regimes, drawing on language possibilities that can cross, challenge, and unravel hostile conditions. They are constantly inventing, (dis)inventing, redefining and reconstructing language to meet their needs and goals, and thus constantly engaged in the discursive (dis)invention of identity and the (dis)invention of language.

2

CROSSCULTURAL VIBRATIONS

The shared language of
contestation of Jamaican Dancehallas
and American Hiphoppas

With the continuum from the Burrus to the beat-boxes, the griots to the DJs
(or MCs), we find not simply the resilience of the African oral tradition;
certainly this is the case, yet all too often a monolithic "African oral tradition"
is evoked as a crude and romantic answer to diasporan complexities. Also at
work here is a conscious attempt on the part of sound culture to force new
technologies to address forms of knowledge that are precolonial in origin but
continually produced and modified by a racist system in which [Anglocentric]
literacy is a privilege and the written word the signified of official (white or
elite) culture.

(Chude-Sokei, 1997: 194)

The paradigm shift of "African Diaspora" from signifying cultural survivals,
commonalities and continuities to denoting cultural hybridization, difference
and discontinuities reflects the new conditions of globalization.

(Sharpe, 2003: 440)

A specially interesting crew turned up at Madam's—West Indian people from
Jamaica mostly. Seems they were regulars. They loved to sing, so did Madam.
Folksongs they called it . . . There were times when there was a great dispute.
"But Madam that's our song" or "Fellows where'd you hear that. That's ours"
and battle royal went back and forth with Madam telling how far in her distant
past she had heard it and it couldn't be West Indian, "Who carried it to you?,"
and they would counter in a similar vein.

(Brodber, 1994: 84–5)

The blues had Mississippi, jazz had New Orleans. Hip-hop has Jamaica.
(Chang, 2005: 22)

The shifting terrains, experiences, aesthetics, and histories that brought about
Hiphop and Dancehall go "back, back and forth and forth" as the epigraphs that
frame this chapter suggest. Chude-Sokei points to the precolonial forms of knowledge, borne in sound culture, that displaced African descendants continuously

employ as they force Western technologies and concepts to engage their experiences of contact with racist systems which privilege Anglocentric literacy and lifestyles. Because enslavers tried so hard to crush many of the African ways of knowing and being, emphasis has been on survivals and continuities, minimizing diasporic complexities. Sharpe alerts us to the paradigm shift from survivals to an emphasis on hybridity, difference, and discontinuities that usher forth with globalization—the mobility of capital, labor, technology, goods, culture, and media images, that "indigenises" metropolitan culture to different people differently. (Blommaert, 2003; Sharpe, 2003) Brodber brings to the fore the inextricable kinship of the oral cultures of Jamaicans and African Americans. There are more shared aspects of African American and African Jamaican expressive cultures than it would first appear.

The shared language and culture of Jamaicans and African Americans has been taken up by linguists,[1] anthropologists/folklorists,[2] and literary and cultural studies scholars and critics,[3] to name a few. A balanced study of the discourses of African American Hiphop and African Jamaican Dancehall should shed light on African influences on diasporic complexities, slavery, colonialization, and the influences of globalization. I approach the task at hand by focusing on what Walter Ong (1982/2002: 11) terms secondary oral cultures—cultures in today's highly technological societies, "in which a new orality is sustained by telephone, radio, television, and other electronic devices that depend for their existence and functioning on writing and print."[4] Thus, this study considers rap and Dancehall music, song lyrics, themes addressed in these lyrics, diffusion and commentary about such via electronic and digital media, such as CDs, the Internet, cable, music videos, and Hiphop and Dancehall magazines to uncover the crosscultural, discursive and linguistic aspects of their discourse and literacy practices. The primary data on which this study is based derive from current recordings of Dancehall and Hiphop artists, from the late 1990s through 2005. The centerpiece of this analysis is of shared vocabulary of these groups. What I mean by shared vocabulary, or lexicon, basically refers to language that each group borrows from the other or that came into the vocabulary of both groups through their experiences of the African background, slavery in the Americas, resistance to systems of oppression, technology, or other social phenomena. I have sought to contextualize such vocabulary against the backdrop of significant social movements and episodes in the history of both groups. For the most part, the words and phrases are grouped following these broad outlines. I have also sought to identify some of the language usage within a framework of known principles in sociolinguistics, such as language crossing. Admittedly, studying so-called secondary oral cultures in this manner is reductive. It uproots the performances out of their primary cultural contexts, and can cause more harm than good. (See Devonish, 1996.) I hope that this work on Hiphop and Dancehall discourse contributes to understanding certain aspects of the shared background of these cultures as well as their cultural creativity.

Jamaican Dancehall artists for the purposes of this study are DJs who are marketing themselves as such and who are generally accepted as Dancehall DJs.

Similarly, Hiphop artists are those MCs who market themselves as such and are known generally as rap artists. To supplement my analysis, I interviewed Jamaican and African American Language (AAL) speakers. Further, I consulted several authoritative sources.[5] Many of the words that I will present here are not new but have been given new meanings. On the other hand, some of the words are staples of the Black experiences of these groups.

Beginning around the 1930s, Jamaicans became increasingly influenced by American popular music with the return of migrant workers from North America, acquisition of radios, telecommunication devices, stereos, records, and exposure to American missionaries. (Stolzoff, 2000: 36) African American music, from gospel, jazz, soul, blues, to R&B, has had an influence on the production of Jamaican musical genres such as Jamaican R&B, ska, and currently Dancehall. Catering to the tastes of Jamaica's elite and middle-class, radio would only play White American and British music. The sound systems provided access to the African American music with which Jamaicans identified. (Chang and Chen, 1998) "The people had to develop their own institutions, called Sound Systems, where the music of Jamaica and [B]lack America could be played without restraint." (Campbell, 1988: 127) Often I have heard it said that African Americans completely ignored reggae during the Bob Marley era. What is usually overlooked in such discussions is that "back in the day" many large U.S. cities, such as Cleveland, Ohio, had small Jamaican communities. However, today there is a visible Jamaican community in places like Cleveland—numbering around 8,518, with Jamaican stores, restaurants, associations, parties, DJs, and some radio programming, though insufficient and hardly equivalent to rap programming. (Bernstein, 2001) In the U.S. the trend remains that reggae music is heard more consistently in cities with larger Caribbean populations via reggae radio shows and in clubs.

One transplanted yardie,[6] Herc, brought the noise from Jamaica to the Bronx, putting together a powerful Sound System, encouraging the MCs to voice over the break beats to keep the party rocking, passing the MC the mic so he could do his thing on the wheels of steel. Through the Jamaican Sound System, in which a selector played records via a turntable with huge amplified speakers and a radio, the DJs, influenced by American deejays, "introduced songs employing the latest jive." Dub versions of songs are created by removing the vocals, leaving the bass, rhythm, and room "for a skillful lyricist [DJ] to throw his own catchy words and phrases on top of the [riddim] at the appropriate moments" (Fernando, 1994: 37).[7] Nowadays, it is normal to hear Dancehall DJs over Hiphop Beats and rappers over Dancehall beats. Collaborations between artists have grown steadily, reflecting and contributing to the crosscultural fertilization of African American and African Jamaican discourse.

But what is African American discourse? What is its relationship to Hiphop discourse? Similarly, what is African Jamaican discourse? And Dancehall discourse? How do these "cultures in [or entangled with] Babylon" (Carby, 1999) relate to one another?

Hiphop and Dancehall discourse

The African American discourse community consists of people of Black African descent born in the United States of America or those who have been socialized into the discourse in a formative way. This does not mean that only one discourse functions among 90 percent of African Americans. It means that there are African American discourses (that exist among other discourses) that function as primary discourses among this population in significant ways. I understand discourse as a system of "behaving, interacting, valuing, thinking, believing, speaking, and often reading and writing that are accepted as instantiations of particular roles . . . by specific groups of people." (Adapted from Gee, 1996: viii) A primary language of this discourse community is African American Language (AAL), which developed as a result of blending European American English with patterns from West African Languages.[8] "The result of this blend was a communication system that functioned as both a resistance language and a linguistic bond of cultural and racial solidarity for those born under the lash [slavery]" (Smitherman, 1987/2000: 272) and its continuing phases of imperialism. As with any group, the discourse practices of African Americans extend throughout all spheres of their lived experiences. Hiphop discourse derives from AAL and also extends it. Smitherman (1987/2000: 242) explains that the verbal art of Hiphop can be defined as a part of the "Black Verbal Tradition—talk-singing, signifying, blending reality and fiction. A contemporary Black response to conditions of joblessness, poverty, and disempowerment." AAL speakers largely provide the language of Hiphop, with some words donated from Spanish, Caribbean Englishes, and graffiti vocabulary. It is graphic and brash, and it adheres to the pronunciation and grammar of AAL. (Smitherman, 1994) The American version of Hiphop mixes Anglocentric literacies with African American literacies to create the dynamic literacies of Hiphop, a merger of Black oral tradition and "stray technological parts intended for cultural and industrial trash heaps," transformed "into sources of pleasure and power." (Rose, 1994a: 71) African American, Carribean, and Latino youth of 1970s New York City found themselves in a nearly bankrupt city, in the poorest neighborhoods, in the poorest-funded school districts, yet in a land of plenty. Hiphop ideology is partly a response to Reagan/Bush-era ideologies of social and civic abandonment of inner-city communities. (Morgan, 2001) Morgan shrewdly assesses Hiphop as "a new form of youth socialization that explicitly addresses racism, sexism, capitalism, and morality in ways that simultaneously expose, exploit, and critique these practices." (Morgan, 2001: 190) This rhetorical situation shaped the production and creation of Hiphop, which is itself a product of all the musics that preceded it: spirituals, blues, be bop, jazz, gospel, rock & roll, R&B/Soul, Dancehall reggae, and others through sampling and mixing.

Though Hiphop is conventionally defined as rapping, deejaying, graffiti writing, and break dancing, in his poll of 800,000 people around the world, Hiphop veteran MC KRS-One (1999) collected nine elements: "1) graffiti art, 2) Djaying (Emceeing/Rapping), 3) break beat, 4) break dancing, 5) beat boxing, 6) street fashion, 7) street language, 8) street knowledge, and 9) street entrepreneurism." Further expanding on the elements of Hiphop, Pough (2004) explains that we can now speak of raptivists, Hiphop actors, Hiphop cinema, Hiphop-inspired poetry and literature, and of course digital Hiphop, as music technology, music videos, video games (e.g., 50 Cent Bulletproof, Def Jam Fight for New York, among others), streaming audio, Internet radio, chat rooms, and websites provide spaces to see, hear, interact with, download, discuss, and co-create aspects of the culture. Hiphop's expansiveness reminds us that it is deeply engaged with mainstream culture and dominant discourses, as hybrid discourses almost always already are.

It is important to view Hiphop as a total culture (albeit a subculture within larger African American culture). The music and lyrics must be considered in relation to beliefs, values, mores, economics, and the complex ideologies of race, class, gender, sexuality, and other social categories that underlie the street apparel, hard body imagery, and the wielding of various symbols. In addition to the global diffusion/distribution of the music, the music industry also plays a large role in shaping this music. Though rap music is the largest-selling music and has crossed over, within the industry itself, the music is held at bay within "Black Music Divisions" and Black executives are only as hot as their latest hot act. They don't get to shape the direction of the music in the same way as White music executives do. The industry does not invest in the music and the communities of the artists. (Negus, 2004) Even still, there are several varieties of rap music reflecting "Black stylings . . . The lyrics come out of the life histories, the everydayness" of Black youth experiences. (Spady and Eure, 1991: 149) Westcoast, Eastcoast, Midwest, and Durty South represent general styles, which can encompass varieties such as nation conscious/Afrocentric rap, hardcore/gangsta, message, street conscious, bohemian experimentalism, party/pop, love, or battle rhyming, to name a few.

Similarly, the African Jamaican discourse community refers to those Jamaicans of Black African descent born in the country of Jamaica or socialized in a formative way into the discourse. As with African Americans, I use the concept of discourse community to refer to the ways that African Jamaicans as a specific group of people make sense out of the world. Thus, African Jamaican discourse encompasses ways of behaving, interacting, valuing, thinking, believing, speaking, reading, and writing, as an African Jamaican person. The primary language acquired by most Jamaicans is Jamaican creole or "patwa" (patois), hereafter Jamaican. (Christie, 2003) Most speakers of Jamaican are descendants of West African people who were enslaved in the seventeenth, eighteenth, and nineteenth centuries, first by the Spaniards, who were relieved of their reign in 1655 by the conquering British.[9] The overwhelming vocabulary of Jamaican is English. The language of the Rastafarian movement, Dread Talk, has been significantly incorporated into Jamaican. Dread Talk is a system of creative word play that adjusts words to create reality from the speaker's point of view. As Pollard (2000: xiii) explains, Dread Talk "reflects the speaker's resistance to perceived oppression (both historical colonial prejudice and current economic disenfranchisement) and the sense of the overwhelming potential spiritual redemption that Rastas can achieve." Dread Talk is important to an ovahstandin of Jamaican Dancehall music because many of the DJs are influenced by Rasta ideology and symbology.

Also comprising Jamaican is a host of African words and communication continuities, with a smattering of Spanish, Portuguese, and French. Jamaican evinces a unique syntax, much of it similar to that of West African languages, and can be considered a language in its own right. It also shares characteristics with other creole languages (Gullah, Krio, Guyanese, among others). (Alleyne, 1980) Jamaican defines itself against English, challenging its dominance as the proper representation of identity for Jamaicans. (Cooper, 2004) Much of the Jamaican oral tradition, themes, cultural practices, and verbal techniques, such as throwing words ("act of casting aspersions without naming the object of abuse" (Cooper, 1995: 6), akin to African American signifying), proverbial rhetoric, liriks, "the enigmatic indirection of riddle and the antiphonal repetitions of oral narration which recur as set linguistic formulations in folk-tale, legend, song-text and performance poetry" (Cooper, 1995: 2), arises from both African oral traditions and the power relations and conditions of slavery and its legacy.

Dancehall discourse derives from this larger Jamaican discourse system. Dancehall is an important field of "active cultural production . . . by which so-called lower class [African Jamaican] youth articulate and project a distinct identity in local, national, and global contexts." (Stolzoff 2000: 1) This genre of Jamaican music emerged within the particular historical, cultural, and material conditions of Jamaica, ravaged by economic exploitation, in communities that had been systematically disenfranchised. Within these oppressive confines, Dancehall music enabled its practitioners to appropriate alternative cultural space, within which they could continue their resistance to the politics of downpression. Dancehall music is a form of reggae. The music is largely digitally produced and incorporates Jamaican folk musics. With the passing of Marley and other greats of his era whose style of reggae deeply reflected their fundamental Rastafarian beliefs and African roots ideology, coupled with political party rivalry and the division of the Black lower class, a rift emerged that was filled by a new local Dancehall reggae style. Dancehall encompasses DJing—chattin pon de mic, toasting, singjaying, Sound System, sound clash, dance, fashion, theatre, modeling, videos, and Dancehall queen contests. Stanley-Niaah (2004: 104) conceptualizes Dancehall as: "A system that can be disaggregated into the particularity of its space, music, song, dance, fashion, language, art, embodied meanings, performance practice, attitude, politics, economy/industry, and style." Drawing on Benitez-Rojo, Stanley-Niaah underscores the fact that there is "a certain way of doing things," especially in the Dancehall, but also throughout Caribbean culture. This is true of most ethnic groups: however, style carries more weight in the carrying out of acts in the Caribbean. This is also true of African American culture.

There are several varieties of Dancehall DJing, including rasta (roots/cultural content), slackness (explicit sexual content), gun lyrics, sound clash (similar to battle rhyming or dis rap), among others. Any song can cross styles. Digital, electronic, and cable media, Internet technology, the music industry, the tourist industry, and immigration have made it possible for this music and other forms, such as passa passa stage plays and theatre, to transcend their geographical boundaries.

There are significant differences between African Americans and African Jamaicans. Whereas the traditional Black church in America has been the major institution that nurtured the primary oral traditions of African Americans, they have been integrated (at least theoretically) into Anglo American values and society via education, media, and everyday life. African Jamaicans, on the other hand, have been able to retain much more of their primary oral cultural characteristics due to a degree of insulation, way of life, natural resources, climate, and economy. Writing of "Jazz and the West Indian Novel" in the late 1960s, Kamau Brathwaite (1993) identifies a few major differences. The West Indian Black deals with "subtleties of caste and colour" and is not a minority, while the American Black is a minority in a White majority. The West Indian slavery experience was different from the American Blacks' enslavement in the South. Particular circumstances in which the enslaved peoples found themselves in the so-called New World, the extent to which the controlling class interfered, the social and environmental conditions would affect their lifeways. Nonetheless, the shared vocabulary of African American and African Jamaican artists represents the various strands of our collective history and experience—including the shared West African background, slavery, radical movements for diasporic Black liberation, post-industrialization, migration, technological diffusion of Black music around the globe via radio, CDs and, of late, cable television and Internet.

The words in Table 2.1 are those that have been given new meaning through Hiphop and Dancehall, or that evolved directly from those cultures. For example, the words "massive," "selecta," and "sound boy" are elements of Dancehall that have evolved through the culture. Though "massive" and "selector" had their function in Standard English, they have been semantically widened and given new meanings distinct to Dancehall. "Sound boy" would be considered a new word that did not exist before the Sound System, which is central to Dancehall. Similarly, "big up," "mash it up," and "nuff respect" were perhaps in usage in Jamaican discourse before Dancehall but have become central in the Dancehall paradigm. The Hiphop parallel to Dancehall's "massive" is "crew," with "represent" being a related foundational concept. The concept and practice of representin is a part of the larger Black discourse that emerged in the slavery experience. Representin is a form of fictive kinship which enslaved Africans devised as a way of surviving, achieving prestige, and creating a Black human identity apart from dehumanized slave. Consonant with the fictive kinship ideology, Black people performed in a manner that protected the humanity of the collective enslaved community. As Signithia Fordham (1996: 75) explains, "in contexts controlled by (an) Other, it was necessary to behave as a collective Black Self while suppressing the desire to promote the individual Self." Cooper's (1995) work on Louise Bennett's proverb usage attests to the fictive kinship/representin practices in the Jamaican context. Though Cooper does not discuss this sociolinguistic accommodation as representin, Bennett's political decision to affirm "naygocentric/nativist aesthetic values, rooted in the particular socio-political contradictions of Jamaican history" (Cooper, 1995: 40–1) is a form of respresentin or fictive kinship. Mintz and Price's (1992: 39) discussion of slave institutions which operated within the parameters of the masters' monopoly of power, but separate from the masters' institutions offers an example of fictive kinship or representin, as they recount an episode reported in Phillippo's *Jamaica, Its Past and Present State* (1834): "[A slave mother beats] her child for telling an overseer where a fugitive slave had run: 'Next time buckra ax you which side neger run, you tell him me no know, massa.'" Thus, representin is a worldview that permits an affinity with other selves seen as similarly situated, regardless of social class. One subscribing to this worldview understands an integral aspect of the lived experiences of group members and can therefore perform in such a way that projects or protects the humanity and complex social situatedness of that group. These concepts are at the center of the alternate worldviews, ways of knowing, recognizing, doing, and being in the world expressed through Dancehall and Hiphop. The sharing of certain core aesthetics, a core theme of this chapter, is evident in Jamaican Dancehall and American Hiphop. For example, Dancehall's "nuff respect" parallels Hiphop's "props"—both terms acknowledging that first and foremost persons from these backgrounds deserve respect and have something of value to offer, so should be accorded recognition, status, and acknowledgement of their excellence. On the other hand, being "wack" means that one's performance of a certain aspect of the culture needs work. Respect and recognition in Black resistance cultures are highly coded. Hiphop terms such as "get crunked" would be considered a new word, while "perculate" is not new but has been employed in a totally new context to refer to a dance with jerky and perhaps perky energetic movement, as coffee in a percolator. Table 2.1 displays fifteen words and phrases that evolved from the cultures of Hiphop and Dancehall and that are shared among these discourse communities.

These terms are very familiar to both Hiphoppas and Dancehallas. They appear in many lyrics. However, transparency is not at issue with the next set of words.

One concept that helps us to discuss the instances of shared vocabulary displayed in Table 2.2 is language crossing—when speakers use a language or style which is not usually considered theirs and they do so for conscious effect. (Rampton, 1995) In this particular grouping of words, African American rappers are using terms that are easily identifiable as Jamaican in order to enjoy attributes accorded to Jamaican DJs. The rappers may do so to appear more hardcore, stylish, in touch

Table 2.1 Words evolving from or associated with the cultures of Dancehall and Hiphop

big up	crew	flow
get crunked	Hiphop	hype
massive	mash it up	nuff respect
perculate	props	represent
selecta	sound boy	wack

with their Black/African consciousness, or to seem cosmopolitan. Performativity is another way this type of language use could be discussed. Performative language use allows a speaker/artist to accomplish something such as "being thought of in a certain way" by sounding a certain way. In some sense most of the words in this entire study could be said to be acts of performativity or identity, meaning that one or the other group is associated with some quality, some things, some places, or some ideas and the other group uses its words to be associated with these things. However, when the quality, thing, place or idea becomes fully integrated into the group's repertoire and associated with the group, the word associated with it is no longer really a crossing. The items in Table 2.2 appeared in this data to be performed as crossings, with African Americans performing items recognizably Jamaican, for the most part.

Table 2.2 displays one African American content phrase, "do rag," nineteen Jamaican content items, four Jamaican function words—"fi," "inna," "me," and "pon"—and three embedded items—"ackee and saltfish," "brown stew chicken," "whole a dem"—shared by Hiphoppas and Dancehallas. Content words refer to specific persons, places or things, often nouns, such as callaloo, mon, gyal, do rag, bwoy, backside, wine etc., but also verbs (bawlin, tief, mash up, reach, sekkle), adjectives (likkle, vex), and adverbs. Embedded items refer to longer stretches of language (ackee and saltfish, brown stew chicken, whole-a-dem) which appear as set phrases. African American "do rag" has come to be a symbol of style. Smitherman (2000: 45) indicates that the phrase comes out of the process/perm era, when brothas had their hair conked. "Do rags" went on to be used by brothas

Table 2.2 Performative/language crossings

Embedded items	Content words	Function words
ackee and saltfish	bawlin	a fi/haffi
brown stew chicken	baxside/backside	a go
whole-a-dem	bwoy	fi
	callaloo	inna
	check for	me
	do rag	nah
	gyal	pon
	gwaan	
	likkle	
	mon	
	mash up	
	reach	
	sekkle	
	tief	
	ting	
	vex	
	wine	

for natural wave styles. (See Appendix.) Nowadays, even White boys sport do rags as a symbol of their being "down wit" Hiphop. "Bwoy" may be a special case, where certain Hiphoppas, particularly those from the South, such as OutKast and Crime Mob, are not borrowing the Jamaican form "boy." The form may be native to the South. In Jamaican, 'boy' is prounounced "bwai." Among performers such as OutKast and Crime Mob the form is used variably with no apparent desire to style or perform characteristics accorded to Jamaican. On the other hand, I have examples from Lauryn Hill, Q Tip, East Coast rappers who appear to be styling.[10]

Precolonial and enslavement mix

We have already alluded to the importance of the slavery experience to AAL and Jamaican. The precolonial background of AAL and Jamaican reveals several language practices that are common to West African languages: no /th/ sound; linguistic reversal; use of proverbs that are a part of the Hiphop/Dancehall mix.[11]

The enslavement context of Africans in the West Indies and the North American South permits some shared language patterns in what became AAL ("Black English"), "Gullah," and Jamaican. Alleyne, writing about the shared African inputs among Afro-American languages and the history behind them, writes:

> The impetus for the settlement of the Carolinas also came from Barbados. In 1670 Spain ceded Charlestown to England, and the whole area began to be colonized slowly by Britishers from the North American colonies, from the West Indies, and from England and Ireland. Slaves came either from the West Indies or directly from Africa. By 1708 the number of slaves almost equaled the number of Whites in the province of South Carolina . . . and by the close of the colonial period the proportion of Blacks to Whites was always much greater. In 1860 the slave population of the Beaufort district was 81.2 percent of the total, a proportion exceeded only by one county of South Carolina—that of Georgetown—and by few others in the entire South.
>
> (Alleyne, 1980: 23–4)

This background suggests that certain words and sounds of African Americans and Jamaicans may not be borrowed but may belong to the mutual stock available to Africans in contact through slavery in the Black Atlantic triangle. Olaudah Equiano's life and text help us to see this. As an enslaved and later freed seaman, he spent ample time in the West Indies, traveling from island to island to various market and plantation centers in Carolina and Georgia, interacting with Africans, both the "seasoned" and freshly enslaved "cargoes." Though he spoke English very well, he was multilingual without question, having in his repertoire the language of his countrymen (of Benin and Eboe), Caribbean languages, the languages of Blacks in Carolina and Georgia, and perhaps others. To clarify my meaning, let's look at the word "jook." Defining this word from the African American context, Smitherman (2000a: 182–3) notes that it comes from Wolof ("dzug") and Bambara "dzugu," meaning "to act disorderly, unruly," and "wicked," respectively. Smitherman's definitions correspond to Lorenzo Turner's (1969: 195) listings of "jug" and "jugu" as Africanisms in Gullah. In the American Old South context, the word referred to dancing, the places where the dances were held or that had a jukebox, after-hours joints, "low dive," or houses of ill-repute. Mostly in spaces outside of the White gaze, the jook joint arose after slavery. Hazzard-Gordon (1990) asserts that the jook joint is the first secular cultural institution of African Americans. It was rooted in West African traditions combining sacred and secular practices. *Vibe* magazine's "Slanguistics" column (August 2004: 44) gives the following current definition: "juke," a verb, "To dance closely with a partner in a sexually provocative manner. R. Kelly is 'jukin' all night' on 'Ignition-Remix.'" The magazine also cites an example showing "juke" as a kind of dance from Kanye West's "The New Workout Plan." Juke box is derived from jook joint. Defining this word from the African Jamaican context, the *Dictionary of Jamaican English* (Cassidy and Le Page, 2002: 253) traces it to Fulani jukka, meaning "spur, poke; knock down" and also to Cameroon pidgin "čuk used to mean 'pierce, prick' . . . In one of the senses, it is noted that these movements are 'usually done suddenly.'" Also of interest here is Cassidy and Le Page's notation of the vulgar usage: "To have sexual intercourse with (a woman)." Contemporary Dancehall reggae artist Elephant Man has a tune entitled "Jook Gal." In the "Head Gawn" remix and video, he collaborates with Jamaican sing-jay Kiprich and African American rappers Twista and the Youngbloodz. In the video, Elephant and his crew meet up with Twista and the Youngbloodz, supposedly in the Durty South. It is no mistake that the meeting place is "Jook Gal's Jook Joint" and the landscape is a rural Southern location resembling a Jamaican rural area, replete with an older Black American man playing a banjo, strumming "Yankee Doodle." Inside, the jook joint (a barn with bales of hay) contains an overabundance of beautiful, sexy Black women, some wearing cowgirl hats and boots, many in short shorts, short skirts, close-fitting pants, and colorful sexy tops, all dancing the jook dance, "winin" (winding), gyrating their waists, hips, and backsides ecstatically.

The nine words/phrases in Table 2.3 below reflect words and language practices influenced by West African languages. They are divided into the following—lexical, phonological, morphological/reduplication, semantic inversion/reversal, sacred/secular, and proverbs. The words in the lexical column came into AAL and Jamaican from an African language. "Jook" has already been mentioned. Dalby (1970) indicates that "boogie woogie" was originally a sexual reference in an African language that transferred into the music domain of Black discourse. "Boogie down" continues this legacy. WAL phonology refers to English words that reflect West African sound patterns (no th sound—yielding dat/dem/dis). Further, a form such as "dem boys" resembles noun plurality in many African languages which is achieved by affixing a third-person plural pronoun. Dalby notes that this form has coalesced with White dialects. In the WAL reduplication/morphology column, I list samples of words that reflect a West African sound/meaning pattern such as

Table 2.3 West African-influenced words and language practices in Dancehall and Hiphop

WAL lexical	WAL phonological	WAL reduplication	Semantic inversion	Sacred/secular	Proverbs
			bad		
jook					Dem Belly Full
boogie down		chi chi			
	dat/dem/dis				
		don **dada**			
				Lord have mercy	
			wicked		

"tyítyi," meaning small size in Ewe, resembling the Jamaican word "chichi," showing reduplication (repetition of the root of a word). The meaning of "chichi" has been extended to homosexual. (See Appendix.) "Dada," as in "don dada," also reflects reduplication influence from a WAL, such as Fante. (See Cassidy and Le Page, 2002: 141.) "Dada" is a term of respectful address. WAL linguistic reversal or semantic inversion refers to use of positive words with negative meaning, while also retaining the negative meaning. (See Smitherman, 1977/1986: 44.) Sacred/ secular refers to the unity of the spiritual and the material as in West African cultures. For example, spiritual language or practices used in "secular domains" or songs. (Smitherman, 1977/1986: 44.) The proverb category indexes the practice in West African and West African-influenced cultures where proverbs are used in more life domains and more extensively than in Western culture, although their usage declines among West African descendants in constant contact with Western cultures. (See Smitherman, 1987/2000.)

Table 2.4 below presents four words that are a result of contact between African Jamaicans/African Americans and speakers of English or another colonial language through the slavery experience.

Major (1970/1994: 36–7) indicates that "bitch" began among North American Africans in the 1800s. For other cultural groups (of non-African descent), "bitch"

Table 2.4 Words evolving from slavery

bitch
muthafucka/muddafucka
nigga
pickaninny/pickney

referred variously to a dog, a type of makeshift lamp, a woman in general, a prostitute, or something difficult to accomplish. "But black speakers have used this word to refer either specifically to mean-spirited women in the [street] life or more commonly (in a nonmalicious way) to refer to any woman; or to flaunting male homosexuals. It is also used to refer to any difficult or formidable situation or person." These usages parallel those in the Jamaican context. However, in popular music, African American artists use the term much more extensively. Major (1970/1994: 310) locates the term "muthafucka" in the 1790s, as "a profane form of address; a white man; any man; anybody; of black origin; sometimes derogatory, sometimes used affectionately; other times used playfully." (See Appendix.) As for "nigga," in the North American context, Major (1970/1994: 319) indicates that the term came into use in the 1620s. There are confusing accounts of the term's origins and meaning. One of Major's sources indicates that it came from "negar," Irish dialect pronunciation of the Spanish word "negro," and that the term was used pejoratively to refer to African Americans. Randall Kennedy (2002: 4) claims that "nigger is derived from the Latin word for the color black, niger." His sources indicate that the word did not originally have negative racist meanings. Smitherman (2006) concurs that "nigger" did not become a racial slur until the nineteenth century. She explains that the three N words—negro, nigger, and nigga—all derive from the same origin: "They made their way into English by way of Latin (niger/nigra/nigrum, 'black or dark-colored'), Spanish and Portuguese (negro, 'black'), and French (negre, 'black')." In the Jamaican context, Cassidy and Le Page (2002) indicate that the term "nayga" arose in the seventeenth century (from the English "neger," influenced from Spanish "negro") and that Jamaicans did not accept White usage. Cassidy and Le Page also indicate that among African Jamaicans the term generally has a negative meaning. However, there is evidence to suggest that the use of "nigga/nayga" among Jamaicans and African Americans has a long history of oppositional in-group usage, though the term is still controversial among members of these discourse communities. Some Black people do not accept usage from anyone. (Check out Capleton's "Dangerous/Who Yuh Callin Nigga?" [mixtape])

The West African language practice of linguistic inversion is reflected in "nigga/nayga." Among some African Americans and African Jamaicans the term can be an endearing reference. It can also refer to a strong, self-determined Black person, one who will not bow to dominant White standards. Smitherman's (1998: 221) historical explanation of "90s niggaz" explains this tradition of resistance in Black cultures: "bad niggaz were fearless, powerful slaves. They dared to buck Ol Massa 'the slave master', they didn't take no shit from Blacks or Whites, and some of them even lived to tell about it." A Jamaican poem by Louise Bennett, "Him Deh Yah" (1966/1995: 39), about Paul Robeson's visit and performance in Jamaica, gives an example of "nayga" as empowering:

An wen him done, de clappin an
De cheerin' from de crowd!

An every **nayga** head swell, every
Nayga heart fell proud!

Bennett glosses "nayga" as "negro" or "nigger."

In the African American context, Major (1970/1994) indicates that around the 1650s "pickaninny" emerged in the old slave states to refer to a Black child. This term has definitely fallen out of usage in AAL. I only found it used poetically in the lyrics of Nas. (See Appendix.) In the Jamaican context, Cassidy and Le Page (2002), as well as the *Oxford English Dictionary*, indicate that "pickney" can be traced to roughly this same time period. These sources suggest that "pickney" probably derives from Portuguese and African pidgin Englishes, such as Cameroon or Sierra Leone. In the Jamaican context, pickney can refer to a child of any race. (See Appendix.) The term is very common in the Jamaican context, as evident in a current tune, "Mr. Teki Baak," by a ba-ad Jamaican sista, DJ Macka Diamond: "you tek everyting why not tek your pickney . . ."

Black strugglers' mix

The Pan-African teachings of Marcus Garvey helped African Jamaicans and African Americans to recognize the connected aspects of their social, economic, cultural, and political struggles. Garvey was born in 1887, while Jamaica was still a British colony. He claimed Maroon ancestry. The Maroons were those Africans who in the seventeenth century escaped to the hills of Jamaica to form their own settlements rather than be enslaved by the Spaniards. (See Cassidy and Le Page, 2002: xl) Founded in Kingston, Jamaica, in 1914, Garvey established the New York base of the Universal Negro Improvement Association (UNIA) in 1917. Garvey was himself influenced by the great African American leader Booker T. Washington, with his example of building Black institutions. Faced with the task of shaping a unified vision of repatriation to Africa for all Africans throughout the diaspora, Garvey's rhetoric included language such as "Grande Nation," used almost as a synonym for Negro; "Race Power," used to remind Black people of Africans' contributions to world culture and that they were once kings, queens, and great rulers; the call to action "Up you mighty race, you can accomplish what you will"; "Africa for Africans, those at home and those abroad." In addition to his public speeches and parades, he created an outlet for his rhetoric by publishing a newspaper, the *Negro World*, and a magazine, the *Black Man*. Further, Garvey's influence on African Americans was so profound that the Harlem Renaissance was alternatively known as "Literary Garveyism," and figures such as Hurston, Hughes, and McKay published in the the *Negro World*. (See Zips, 1995: 48–51.) The membership of the UNIA was at least two million, and Blacks throughout the West Indies, North and Central America, as well as Africa, were among its numbers. One of Garvey's major accomplishments, even though it was betrayed and maligned, was the Black Star Line steamship company that he and the UNIA created as a vehicle for worldwide commercial trade in the interest of Black people.

African American MCs Mos Def and Talib Kweli named their duo after this revolutionary idea—calling themselves Blackstar.

The Pan-Africanist concepts of Marcus Garvey anchored in the Ethiopian Emperor of Addis Ababa, Haile Selassie I, continues the traditions of Revival African Zionists of the nineteenth century, coupled with the Rastafari movement. Rastafari is very important to the diasporic aesthetic. Involving a religious political philosophy of life, Rastafari critiques the (neo)colonial administration and promotes the liberation of all Africans on the continent and in the diaspora, while advocating African-derived cultural processes, collectivity, and self-sufficiency. "[B]y 1960— an articulate and systematized institution had developed—with its adherents numbering in the thousands around Jamaica with the movement's *words* migrating throughout the African Diaspora." (Niaah, 2003: 835; my emphasis) The attitude and sound of reggae music owe much to Rastafari and Maroon practices. The drumming practices and also the philosophy of word, sound, power have spread throughout aspects of Jamaican culture. The word, sound, power philosophy is akin to Nommo, a precolonial epistemology, retained throughout the diaspora in religious and secular practices. Nommo is the belief and practice that the word has the ability to transform and create reality, a worldview that permeates Afro-American expressive cultures.

In the period around the First World War, Jamaicans were very concerned and engaged in the Black Liberation Movement. Black institutions such as the UNIA and the African Blood Brotherhood (ABB) fostered this consciousness. The ABB was founded by a West Indian immigrant, Cyril Briggs, around 1917. It had posts in the U.S. and the West Indies, and published the *Crusader* as a means of spreading its ideas and alerting its audience to issues about which they should be concerned. (See Kelley, 2002.) Eventually, the ABB broke up because of disagreements over Garvey's policies, internal disagreements with socialist party politics, and rivalry between West Indians and African Americans. The precepts of the ABB centered on self-defense, self-determination, an international perspective on peoples of African descent all over the world. Looking back, we can see that the ABB is ideologically related to the nineteenth-century Black nationalism and self-defense teachings of David Walker and Henry Highland Garnett. Looking forward to the revolutionary Black nationalism of the 1960s, the ABB is precursor to organizations such as the Black Panthers, Republic of New Africa, among others. (See Kuykendall, 2002.) The parallels between race relations in Jamaica and the U.S. are reflected in Black thought and Black movements:

> During the 1960s and 1970s, a more vibrant strain of Black nationalism was to be detected in the Black power movement, advocated in the U.S. by Malcolm X, Stokely Carmichael (Kwame Toure), the Student Non-violent Coordinating Committee [SNCC], and the Black Panther Party. This Black power trend quickly spread throughout the Caribbean.
>
> (Mars, 2004: 567)

Black expressive culture continued to produce art out of adversity, reflecting experiences of oppression, racism, hope, and struggle. For example, Bob Marley and Marcia Griffith's reggae version of the Nina Simone classic "Young Gifted and Black" in 1970 exemplifies the reverberation of Black aesthetics through music in the diaspora. (See Pereira, 1998.) In the African American context, along with the Black Arts Movement and the shift of Black migration to the Northern urban centers, more secularized forms emerged. In the Jamaican context, Dancehall began flourishing around the 1950s, though it certainly was not called "Dancehall" until the nineties.

In the American context, Clarence Major (1970/1994) says that the verbal art of toasting became popular in the 1950s through the 1970s. Abrahams (1970) speculates that the toast might have been present in minstrel shows. He is more certain however that the toasts began at the beginning of the twentieth century and were a riff off the conventional European custom of dedicatory speeches at drinking occasions. The African American toasts were performed around pool halls, on street corners, in prisons, and in other predominantly Black spaces. The canonical African American toasts are longer narrative poems, such as "The Signifying Monkey," "Stagger Lee," and "The Titanic." Smitherman (1977/1986) notes that nearly each rhymed couplet brings the funk that was absent in the older prose narratives about tricksters and bad niggas such as Brer Rabbit or High John. Jemie (2003) explains that values and practices of the badman, such as terrorizing the Black community and its women, that are immortalized in the toasts are a minority as compared to the whole of the tradition of African American orature. Overwhelmingly, unfair social order and unjust law have always been the adversaries in the main of the tradition and in the toasts. Daryl Cumber Dance (2002: 475) gives the following description of the African American toasts:

> Among the most popular African American adult folk rhymes are those long bawdy narrative poems called the toasts. The toasts generally deal with a hero who is "ba-ad," one who violates the laws and moral codes of the larger society but engages in exploits and lives a lifestyle that is celebrated in these verses. He kills without a second thought. He courts death constantly and does not fear dying. He loves flashy clothes and luxury cars. He asserts his manhood through his violent physical deeds and sexual exploits . . . The toasts are a clear precursor of contemporary rap, which usually celebrates the same type of characters, the same lifestyle, and the same exploitation of women. The sexually explicit language and even some of the formulaic lines of the raps seem to be taken directly from the toasts.

Abrahams' study of West Indian patterns of performance (1983) sites toasts in Nevis that have a few of the characteristics of African American toasts, including obscene, boastful, and comical, but that take place at formal occasions such as wedding feasts. Although Abrahams does not discuss toasts in the Jamaican context, the Jamaican tea meeting demonstrates parallel development.

In the late 1970s Dance (1985) collected a short children's rhyming game called "Stagolee." Although the game is not a toast, it stands as a testament to cultural contact and diffusion. Another type of toasting in the Jamaican context is synonymous with DJing (chattin pon de mic), or the ability to "coin lyrics spontaneously." (Williams, n.d.) It is said that early Jamaican DJ Count Matchukie began the practice of rhyming over riddims in the style of African American radio announcers, eventually affecting an original Jamaican style. (Fernando, 1994)

Inherent in this broad sketch of the shared aspects of Jamaican and African American struggle for freedom is the fact that migration, migrant workers, travel, and remittances have played large roles in the exchange of ideas and culture among the two groups. For example, Bob Marley was so deeply affected by the civil unrest he witnessed on a visit to the U.S. that he wrote "Burnin and Lootin".[12] Tables 2.5 and 2.6 show words that emerged from the Black Liberation Movement persisting in Dancehall and Hiphop. Table 2.5 shows fifteen words associated with Rastafari used by Hiphoppas. Table 2.6 shows seventy-two words/phrases associated with the badman/badwoman/outlaw aesthetic, an inherent aspect of Black liberatory imagination. I don't think the influence of the West African practice of sacred/secular duality can be overstated here, as the Black Liberation Movement comprises both sacred and secular forms. Rastafari is a religious and social movement.

It is also important to acknowledge the influence that Hollywood and American gangsterism has had on these cultures. The gangster is an American folk hero as can be understood from the literature and media about the escapades of John Dillinger and others who have been glorified in Hollywood movies (*The Godfather*, *Scarface*, *Carlito's Way*, etc.) and television shows (*The Sopranos*, *The Wire*).

Many of the themes, personas, and scenarios performed in rap follow those of the badman celebrated in the African American toasts. These have been updated with references drawn from contemporary consumer and popular culture. As with African American Hiphop, Jamaican badmanism is a defining characteristic of Dancehall discourse.

> "Badmanism" is a theatrical pose that has been refined in the complicated socialization processes of Jamaican ghetto youth who learn to imitate the sartorial and ideological "style" of the heroes and villains of imported American films. Caribbean societies have a long history of ghetto youth internalizing images of Hollywood heroism and gun violence.
>
> (Cooper, 1994: 430–1)

Table 2.5 Words emerging from the Black Liberation Movement

babylon	baldhead/ed	bredren
dreaded/dread	dreadlock	ital
ganja	Haile Selassie	Jah
ovastan	politrix	rasta
Rastafari	spliff	reggae

Table 2.6 Outlaw/resistance words/sayings

backshots	balla	benz
bimmer	batty boys	bati fies
benjamins	bling bling	blocka blocka
bloodclots	blunt	bomb
booyacka booyacka	bone	boo
booty call	break it down	buckshots
chicken head	chill	chronic
clockin	crib	dealio
diss	dogs	don
don't hate da player/ just hate da game	dough	dro
drops	dude	fly
gangsta	gat	gear
get busy	glock	got it goin on
homie	honies	hood
ice	keep it real	kicks
legit	lick shots	mack daddies
madd	main squeeze	mamma jamma
moe	murderation	o.p.p.
paper	playahate	played
posse	punnani	pushin
pussy boy	rankin	rockin
roll	rude boys	shorty
shottas	shizzle my nizzle	sweat
thugs/tugs	weed	wifey

The shared vocabulary in Table 2.6 can be grouped thus:

- **Badman/badwoman [badgyal]**: balla, boo, don, mack daddies, mamma jamma, rankin, rude boys, thugs, dogs, dude, gangsta, honies, homie, main squeeze, posse, shorty, shottas, and wifey;
- **Gun-related**: booyacka booyacka, buckshots, lickshots, blocka blocka, gat, glock;
- **Verbs/sayings of the game**: break it down, buss, clockin, don't hate da player—just hate da game, drops, got it goin on, rockin, roll, playahate, played, pushin, sweat, tes;
- **Evaluators**: bomb, fly, legit, madd;
- **Status symbols**: benz, bimmer, bling bling, benjamins, crib, dough, gear, kicks, ice, paper, hood;
- **Heterosexistfreedom**: backshots, bone, booty call, o.p.p., punnani;
- **Other(ed) personas**: batty boys, chicken head, pussy boy;
- **Preferred smokes and drinks**: blunt, chronic, dro, moe, weed;
- **Creative language use**: dealio, murderation, shizzle my nizzle;
- **Bad words**: bati fies, blood clots.

The outlaw discourse reveals a wealth of terms and is a double-edged sword. Badmanism comes out of the trickster traditions of these groups which create their own intellectual and cultural property in an effort to resist White supremacy. Dancehallas and Hiphoppas have transformed or transferred these discourses into popular culture and are garnering capital, both economic and cultural, by exploiting "difference." While all the while exploiting these cultural productions, global corporations and their experts denigrate these cultures as representing the downfall of civilization.

Conclusion

There are many other avenues to be explored in this line of research. From an historical perspective, Lalla and D'Costa (1990) mention that a Black American started the first Baptist church in Kingston, Jamaica, in the late 1700s. Other free American Blacks also came to Jamaica with royalists to offer Christian education. This type of contact may have left influences in Jamaican Baptist churches or such religious educators may have brought back Jamaican practices to Americans upon their return. Other questions to be explored are: To what extent are oppression and limited educational opportunities in both America and Jamaica responsible for language and discourse commonalities?

How do the patterns of social exclusion operate in both societies, and how do those patterns of exclusion affect the popular culture/environment produced by the Afro communities in both societies? In terms of linguistic evolution of AAL and Jamaican, how does the urban–rural migration/interaction influence the development of both linguistic traditions? One of the interesting aspects of the American and Jamaican experiences in the twentieth century was the massive migration from the rural areas to urban environments—a process of dislocation/relocation/transposition that has interesting consequences for mainstream culture in both societies. It may be useful to explore the similarities in linguistic influences upon both societies and the interactive effect on Afro communities in both societies, given the encounters in Harlem, Boston, and other major areas in North America over the course of the twentieth century.

In the present exploration of the shared lexicon of Dancehall and Hiphop, we find not only concepts and practices inherited from West Africa but also our collective experiences of slavery and struggles for freedom. Asante (1991) states that an analysis which combines attention to communication styles and folkloristic modalities among Africanized languages reveals the sense of a language more so than mere analysis of retained lexical items in those languages. Brathwaite (1993), writing of Afro-American and Caribbean language, argues that although these Afro-American cultures used English, it was English with an African heritage, what he calls "nation language." Historical memory, deep cultural practices, adaptation to new technologies and social systems, along with resistance to current oppressions, play major roles for these Dancehallas and Hiphoppas in maintaining, developing and creating their worldviews, identities, and means of survival.

3

YOUNG WOMEN AND
CRITICAL HIPHOP LITERACIES

Their readings of the world

Figure 3.1 Missy Elliott billboard

The purpose of this chapter is twofold: to include the voices of African American female adolescents who are reared in this current period of commercial Hiphop culture, how they are represented to themselves in music, images, as these appear in secondary oral contexts—the music video and the hood novel;[1] and to look at the competing and conflicting discourses of Hiphop and dominant cultures.

In this chapter I draw heavily from James Gee's argument on the concept of semiotic domains, as it is helpful to an analysis of how people make sense out of and read the world. "By semiotic domain I mean any set of practices that recruits one or more modalities (e.g., oral or written language, images, equations, symbols, sounds, gestures, graphs, artifacts) to communicate distinctive types of meanings."

(Gee, 2003: 18) Semiotics refers to things that can stand for ideas and take on meanings, "not just words. All of these things are signs . . . that 'stand for' (take on) different meanings in different situations, contexts, practices, cultures, and historical periods." (Gee, 2003: 17) An expression such as "I got your chicken head" is from the semiotic domain of Hiphop. In Hiphop parlance, a chickenhead is not the head of a fowl, but a label that means dumb female. The chicken head is also a dance. In its primary context, the expression "I got your chickenhead" would typify a retort by a Black female (or Latina) who has been called outa her name (been insulted or dissed) and is not havin it (accepting the chickenhead label). You may be able to read lyrics from CD liner notes or from the Internet, or you may transcribe them yourself from rap CDs. However, if you don't know how the words are used within their primary contexts, you cannot read the words and you cannot fully understand Hiphop discourse. As Gee (2003: 18) asserts, "If we think first in terms of semiotic domains and not in terms of reading and writing as traditionally conceived, we can say that people are (or are not) literate (partially or fully) in a domain if they can recognize (the equivalent of 'reading') and/or produce (the equivalent of 'writing') meanings in the domain." The semiotic domain that we will be concerned with in this chapter is Black femalehiphophood. The internal design grammar of Black femalehiphophood consists of "principles and patterns in terms of which one can recognize what is and what is not acceptable or typical content" in Hiphop from an adolescent Black femalehiphop perspective. The external design grammar involves "the principles and patterns in terms of which one can recognize what is and what is not an acceptable or typical social practice and identity in regard to the affinity group" (Gee, 2003: 30), Black females associated with the semiotic domain of Hiphop. This does not mean that all Black females who participate in Hiphop or who identify as Hiphop,[2] think or feel the same way on all issues. Age, social position/ing, sexuality, education, experience, ethnicity are significant variables. I choose Black femalehiphophood rather than Black womanhood and Hiphop because I am looking at the intersection or inextricable relationship of Hiphop consciousness, which is in conversation with Black, dominant, and other discourses, and femalehood, and I wish to illuminate perspectives of the world from Black female teenagers: one is the fictional Winter Santiaga in Sister Souljah's novel *The Coldest Winter Ever* (1999); and three are community youth with whom I work on a regular basis.

I am interested in Hiphop consciousness, how Black youth who identify as Hiphop negotiate themselves when they are represented to themselves in venues of the larger society. KRS-One defines Hiphop expansively as 'a behavior that frees the mind of inner city people.[3] KRS-One (1999) further explains that the language and creative intelligence of Hiphop is "The transformation of subjects and objects in an attempt to describe [a] consciousness," a consciousness that the English language is not fully capable of expressing, hence, Hiphoppas exploit all available means to their own purposes to foreground their experiences. I find KRS-One's definition helpful because it comes from practitioners of the genre and lifestyle. Of the nine elements of Hiphop that KRS-One (1999) collected from Hiphoppas from around the world, "street language," "street knowledge," and "street entrepre-neurism" will be pertinent to the issues discussed in this chapter.[4] Street language and street knowledge and the signifying traditions of Black cultural repertoires, especially, are central in an investigation of Hiphop literacies because one of the basic principles of Hiphop's ideology is to confront officially prescribed or received knowledge with local knowledge. (Morgan, 2001) I use the term "Hiphop literacies" to foreground the ways in which Hiphoppas manipulate as well as read and produce language, gestures, images, material possessions, and people, to position and protect themselves advantageously.

The lifeworld domain is where people experience life, beauty, truth, goodness, evil, etc., based on their structural positions which offer them certain views of reality, deny or offer them access to adequate social goods, deny or offer them certain discourses. As I explained earlier, discourses are ways of being a certain type of person using available resources to present oneself in ways that validate a certain way of being. People internalize or appropriate images, patterns, and words from the social activities in which they have participated. (Gee, 1999)

Streetlife discourse, which is integral to Hiphop consciousness, refers to ways of being, knowing, acting, and/or making a life from a devalued or officially overlooked sector of the lifeworld, the streets. Anglo-American gender ideologies present hegemonic conceptions of manhood and womanhood in almost all life domains and discourses. For females, these ideologies control definitions of who is and who is not a real woman. Hill-Collins (2004: 193) explains:

> All women engage an ideology that deems middle-class, heterosexual, White femininity as normative. In this context, Black femininity as a subordinated gender identity becomes constructed not just in relation to White women, but also in relation to multiple others, namely, all men, sexual outlaws (prostitutes and lesbians), unmarried women, and girls. These benchmarks construct a discourse of a hegemonic (White) femininity that becomes a normative yardstick for all femininities in which Black women typically are relegated to the bottom of the gender hierarchy.

Needless to say, these hegemonic gender ideologies work in tandem with economic, political, and social structures to maintain societal order and control how people view and conduct themselves. These dominating and oppressive discourses are nearly impossible to avoid and manifest themselves in many ways. In engaging with them and simultaneously struggling to avoid them, many Black youth develop codes of conduct, beliefs and practices, self-presentation and language styles. What I strive to point out in this chapter is that youth are aware of the dominating forces but do not possess the critical tools necessary to totally escape internal victim blaming for their predicament. Their awareness of these forces is apparent in what I call street consciousness. Street consciousness enables one to handle a given situation expediently for the (usually short-term) maximum benefit of self. Elites cloak their role in the production of uninsulated streetlife by promoting dominant discourses that profess, among other values, hard work, self-reliance, sacrifice, so-called middle-class values, while maintaining unequal distribution of social goods. For example, we are taught to shun many professions as less respectable than others: prostitution, pornography, stripping, and even certain branches of law, medicine, academia, and certain sports. However, for professions such as prostitution, pornography, or stripping, we do not focus on critiquing the society that produces them. Studies of discourse, power, and knowledge demonstrate that through official institutions such as schools and the media, elites disseminate certain scripts, which create inequality, and value people differently based on White patriarchal market values. These perceptions are continuously reinforced, making the reproduction of unequal society seem natural when in fact unjust social relations are constructed and continuously reinscribed and re-enacted daily through various social practices which are detrimental to the development of just and equal community. (van Dijk, 1993)

One way to think of the lifeworld domain is in relation to these competing discourses. Elijah Anderson (2002: 300) identifies self-presentation as central to survival and avoidance of violence in domains of the lifeworld. Basic human dignity and respect should be a given in society; however, due to the consumer culture in which we live, lives are assigned different values based on their positioning in the social order. Thus, members of socially and racially stigmatized groups have devised ways to earn respect and ways to project their value and knowledge, including: "facial expressions, gait, and verbal expressions . . . [p]hysical appearance, . . . clothes, jewelry, and grooming, . . . [These play] an important part in how a person is viewed."

I turn here to examine how Hiphoppas draw on multi-modal meaning-making systems in the lifeworld domain, how they evaluate and contest ideas in this domain, and how they struggle against hurtful practices of social inequality. The first part of this examination, drawn from Sister Souljah's *The Coldest Winter Ever*, looks more at the signs that represent principles and patterns Winter (the main character) recognizes as (un)acceptable or typical social practice and identity in regard to the affinity group Black femalehiphoppas. The second part of the exploration concentrates mostly, but not solely, on the linguistic resources that the three adolescent Black femalehiphoppas recognize as (un)acceptable or typical social practices and identity to Black femalehiphoppas.

Black femalehiphophood in print: the ghetto girl

I will begin by briefly summarizing the social value of Souljah's text by providing context for the passages that will be analyzed. As stated in the book's dedication, "This novel is dedicated to the era in which we live. The era in which love, loyalty, truth, honor and respect died. Where humility and appreciation are nonexistent. Where families are divided and God reviled. The era. The Coldest Winter Ever." Set in Brooklyn, New York, the time period of the novel is from 1977 to the early

44

2000s. During this era drugs, materialism, and seduction by the so-called American Dream have plagued Black culture. Through this story, Souljah sends a message about life to young Black people, but more directly to young Black females. Her story is about a girlchild in the "promised land," Winter Santiaga, the daughter of Ricky Santiaga, an inner-city drug lord, who becomes successful enough to move out to the suburbs. To the extent of her family structure and function, Winter is raised in a traditional patriarchal American family that includes her father at the helm, mother, and sisters. The family is dysfunctional, however, because its values have been shaped by the market culture into which she was born—obsession with wealth, youth, material possessions, beautiful bodies, defined in relation to Eurocentric norms. As Gwendolyn Pough (2004: 146) explains, "[Winter's] views about success and power stem not only from growing up the daughter of a drug dealer but also from the things that society as a whole values and sees as markers of success."

After her father's dynasty crashes, Winter uses coldhearted codes of conduct of streetlife and the dope game to survive and maintain her wealthy lifestyle. By the novel's end, she is doing a lengthy prison sentence, set up by her drug-dealer boyfriend and one-time friendly girlfriend. Although one of Sister Souljah's main purposes with this novel is to address the Hiphop community and illuminate its collusion in its exploitation, she also exposes the very social systems and practices that continue to warp Black individuals.

In the two *The Coldest Winter Ever* examples, I will focus on the Black female body as the site of competing discourses, which occur within the same body and across Black women, as we will see within Winter herself and between Winter and the social worker.

When the teenaged Winter is placed as a ward of the state, she is interviewed by a social worker about her educational experience and goals. The social worker and Winter signify two Black females situated in different domains of the lifeworld. The social worker represents an educated, middle-class Black woman, a certain type of knowing body. Winter reads the following as signs of the social worker's value and role in the larger society:

> She had her hair pulled back in a neat sweep. Her perm needed a serious touch-up. I could see she tried hard to lay the naps down with some gel that was turning white and flaking. She did her own nails, but believe me she was the type who was too lazy to take off the old layer of polish, so she just piled the new layer on top so it didn't lay smooth on her nails. On her feet were some pleather knockoffs. The kind that when you flipped them over, had a stamp on the bottom that read "man-made uppers." Her pantsuit was JCPenney's or Sears, definitely polyester or rayon.
>
> . . . I checked her left hand. No engagement ring, no wedding ring, nothing. On the wall she had some kind of degree from Fordham University.

. . . I gave her answers, short ones. No sense in getting all involved when she was a walking, talking example of what education amounted to. What was I supposed to do? Struggle to be like her? Pay some big school, big, big money so I could get a little job in some little place making an iddy biddy bit of cash. What do I get? To hang a stupid-ass degree up in my little office where I don't make enough dough to get a regular manicure, pedicure, or perm. I should be interviewing her, asking her what's *her* problem.

. . . She asked me could I read and write. I told her, "Of course, and I can talk too."

(Souljah, 1999: 179–80; original emphasis)

Apparatuses of the state such as the university authorize the social worker, legitimize her knowledge, and confer status upon her. Winter rejects this prescribed way of reading the social worker's status. To Winter, the signs that signify the low-liness of the social worker are: unfashionable hair, scruffy nails, shoes and clothing made from low-quality materials; no jewelry; no husband or significant companion as signified by the absence of a wedding or engagement ring; a low-paying job; and a university plaque. The social worker is represented to herself, or at least to Winter, as someone whose knowledge is debilitating. It doesn't empower her or her community. The social-working-self mediated through market discourse comes up short. From Winter's vantage point, formal education has no tangible value or meaning or significance. It produces people who have been educated away from their own people and trained to serve the interests of the state. The social worker mistakes Winter's rejection of official educational discourse for illiteracy. Winter is a sign of the unknowing body, when in fact she understands all too well that market discourse is the one that counts. Her sarcastic reply to the social worker's questioning of her literacy—"Of course, and I can talk too"—points up the fact that there are, for her, more significant ways of being and knowing which pay bigger dividends.

Winter consumes and embodies another type of knowledge that thwarts her self-development. She says:

To be able to set up your own empire in your neighborhood, or even somebody else's neighborhood for that matter. To buy cars, Jeeps, trucks. To sport the flyest shit made by top designers everyday. To be able to buy property, mansions, and still have apartments on the side. To be able to shit on people before they get a chance to shit on you. That's power. Who could argue with that? A regular nigga worked all week for change to get to work plus a beer to forget about how hard he worked. My pops was a major player for a long time. With the benefit of his knowledge I could make the world kiss my ass, but better than he did 'cause he could now teach me about the mistakes. Let's compare it, ten years of good living

46

and twenty years of high living versus sixty years of scraping to get by. Enough said.

(Souljah, 1999: 192–3)

Market discourse more directly shapes Winter's consciousness and mediates her sense of self. She is represented to herself by her ability to consume power in material forms: cars, Jeeps, trucks, designer clothes, property ownership—control. It is about power for Winter, the power to control a neighborhood. The power to control one's identity, such that one is not perceived as just "a regular nigga," but, if anything, "a bad bitch." Though both Winter and the social worker are parts of the same system, their locations in different sectors of the social hierarchy offer them differing views of reality. Though much of Winter's street consciousness and many of her values coincide with those of the power market culture of America (her pursuit of property, liberty, the American Dream) there is no legitimate institution that authorizes her body of knowledge. She is just another girl out there in the streets, but her life is just as much a part of the social system as is the social worker's. Souljah's insightful hood novel offers an authoritative depiction of the ghetto girl highlighting the implications of dominant social systems and their influences upon the lives of African American females in ways that thwart their development in healthy self-affirming ways.

Some women are and some women ain't: digital Black femalehiphophood

A similar plethora of complicated issues surrounds the consumption of dominant images of Black females in popular media by young Black females. The following examples are drawn from an audiotaped viewing and subsequent discussion of a rap video among three African American females, one aged seventeen and two aged nineteen.[5] The nineteen-year-olds are college students and roommates at a university in central Pennsylvania. They've known each other for approximately two years. The seventeen-year-old is a high-school student in the same region, and the sister of one of the nineteen-year-olds. The other nineteen-year-old was raised on the East Coast, while the sisters are Midwesterners. All of the participants are in the middle-income range and all spent their formative years in Black urban areas. The "rap session" took place in my home. I audiotaped the girls' conversation and responses as the videos played and asked the young women questions at the end of selected videos pertaining to their thoughts surrounding the performances. The "rap session" and viewing of rap videos lasted approximately ninety minutes. I transcribed selected passages of the conversation. As in analysis of the hood novel, I pay particular attention to how the girls make meaning of the images and representations. I also pay attention to the girls' interpretation of song lyrics in the videos and their application of these to their lived experiences and their negotiated reception of these interpretations against dominant and competing constructions of reality.

One of the videos that generated complex discourse was Nelly and the St. Lunatics' "Tip Drill." The St. Lunatics are an extremely popular Midwest, Southern-styled, male, African American rap group. The song and video could be considered a strip club anthem, replete with signs of carnality and status, attractive pulsating young Black women wielding their power signs—their beautiful, shapely bodies—backsides, breasts, lips, tongues, fly hairstyles, varied brown skin tones, stylish (if very little) clothing, heels, nails, vivid colors; and virile men flashing their Black men's power signs—cash money, hard body posturing, gold, jewelry, fine cars, strong drinks, urban apparel. The chorus of the song (chanted by male rappers) presents its theme: "it must be yo ass cause it ain't yo face. I need a tip drill. I need a tip drill." A "tip drill" relates to the performance ritual enacted by strip dancers and their consumers. The objective of the female stripper is to get mostly male consumers to spend large tips, to hold many men under her sway: in so doing, she reigns as a status symbol. The objective of the mostly male consumer is to get female strippers to arouse his sexual imagination. The more women he is able to hold under his sway, the higher his status. The participants—stripper and consumer—exploit every means possible within the limits of strip club protocol to attain their desired goals.

It is readily apparent at the beginning of the conversation that speaker ED's language works to enact the conflicts apparent in Hiphop and dominant discourses. Hiphop discourse values street knowledge and street entrepreneurship, which challenge the dominant values of the equality of all men and women in the ideal of the democratic capitalist economy. To the question "What y'all think about it [the video]?", ED's language re-enacts the dominant perspective when she says "If *you* wanna look at it *in a sense*, like, yeah, *it is degrading to women*," where "you" and "in a sense" mark the perspective as dominant and conflicted.

Judeo-Christian values underlie our dominant American discourse and would shun overtly sexual images and impute chastity, virtue, innocence, heterosexuality, and marriage to the all-American young female. At the same time, the fact remains that the rap video vixen industry thrives on young women looking to earn a decent wage (which is questionable) and perhaps gain an entrée into the movies or music industry by assuming usually subordinate positions in front of or under the camera appearing to embrace sexual abandon. bell hooks (1992: 61–77) candidly calls this "selling hot pussy."

As a young African American woman who feels that she is represented by the males and females in the video, ED counters with: "But then the women had their little part in there too, and showed what *we* do to guys." Hiphop ideology demands that its practitioners "keep it real," speak from their lived experience not an ideal from dominant discourses whether religious, Anglocentric, or Afrocentric. ED authenticates the lives of Black women who strip for a living although she is not a stripper. Her use of the pronoun "we" signals solidarity. Why would ED do this? In Hiphop discourse this is an act of "representin." The concept and practice of representin is a part of the larger Black discourse practice that emerged in the slavery experience and is akin to fictive kinship, wherein enslaved Africans devised a way of surviving, achieving prestige and creating a Black human identity apart from that of dehumanized slave. Consonant with the fictive kinship ideology, Black people performed in a manner that protected the humanity of the collective enslaved community. As Signithia Fordham (1996: 75) explains, "in contexts controlled by (an) Other, it was necessary to behave as a collective Black Self while suppressing the desire to promote the individual Self."

Throughout the session, ED, BE, and ET (co-constructed with me) almost always work to recognize the lives represented in the staged video in terms of local knowledge or the lived experience of Black youth—the "keeping it real" ideology of Hiphop. However, in their quest to keep it real, they also display instances of succumbing to racist stereotypes and controlling myths of Black womanhood. Although this video, promoted by the mostly White corporate-controlled music industry, a typical gangsta rap-styled text, is patriarchal and sexist, the young women struggled to find language to empower themselves through their negotiated reception of it. The following examples are offered as representations of instances in which this occurred.

In Examples One and Two the categories of "stripper" and "tip drill" are juxtaposed with the phrase "girls out here."

Example One

BE: I don't think it's degrading to women. I don't think it's degrading to women. *It's girls out here* who *strippers*. *It's girls out here* who *really tip drills*. Know what Uhm saying?

ET: Yep.

Example Two

ER: What is a tip drill?

BE: A *tip drill* is a *ho* or, well, *I ain't gone say a ho*, I'ma say a *stripper*.

ET: With a ugly face and a big butt.

BE: With a ugly face and a big booty, a bangin body. (Sings song: "It must be yo ass cause it ain't yo face".)

"Girls out here" references the racialized, genderized, classed world that the Black female must navigate to survive. "Ho" is compared with "stripper" and rejected. These usages of language implicate a non-acceptance of the definitiveness of these categories, but at the same time, this labeling that the girls use to make distinctions shows the stratification of the women in the communities that the video represents, showing their simultaneous engagement with dominant and Black discourses. This simultaneous entanglement with dominant and Black aesthetics is apparent also in Example Two, when speakers ET and BE define "tip drill" as "a ugly face and a big butt" (ET); and "ugly face and a big booty, a bangin body (BE)." A well-built woman with a fleshy backside has long been a symbol of health and beauty in

49

African cultures. It symbolized well-being, fertility, and sex appeal. But once appropriated into global market culture, as was the case in slavery and which has continued on until now, the value of the hypersexualized Black body is heightened to such a degree that a face is not even needed: the body produces or sells. The difference is that today, women can be paid for their bodies, even if they do not control the market.

Similarly, Example Three reveals the girls' recognition of the social situatedness of race and gender of Black males and females.

Example Three

ER: Most of those girls. I didn't see any ugly girls in that video.

ET: I did.

BE: Tip drills. I mean. They don't. It's not necessarily a ugly girl. It's just. It's basically a stripper song. That's what that song is. It's a stripper song.

ET: Right.

BE: For girls who get tips. And they sayin. It's lightweight like the niggas [Black male rappers] is sayin, "We got money. We tippin." Know what Uhm sayin. But they also talkin about the girls too. Like, it could mean a lot of different things in the song. I think. I don't think it's degrading to women.

BE recognizes that the males in the video want to be recognized as men by their ability to spend money. She explains: "the niggas is sayin . . . 'We got money. We tippin." In today's global economy, people are recognized and defined by their ability to consume. As Blackness is so highly stigmatized, Black males, as represented in the video, seek to elevate their status through spending money and consumption. In this case, they are consuming Black females that are deemed negative. BE points this out, when she notices that the males criticize the strippers for making money this way when she says: "But they also talkin about the girls too." BE's realization that the guys simultaneously make fun of and make use of the strippers parallels ED's conflicted evaluation of the video strippers when she labels it degrading, yet finds some empowerment in the strippers' signifying on their male customers (when the ladies sang to the men, "It must be yo money cause it ain't yo face, I need a tip drill"). Perhaps the men see these women as a direct affront to their power as breadwinning males. In other words, in all of their femininity, the video women are participating in practices that are gendered male.

BE, ED, and ET discuss the gendered aspects of the performance during their viewing of the video. They take note and comment upon the severity of the ways in which the video girls simulate sex acts that are traditionally thought to be male dominant.

BE: Look how she act like she havin sex with her.

ED: Like she hittin it from the back.

ET: Yeah.

BE: Them the girls that be getting more tips. Guys like that kinda stuff. Look at her. She ri: din. [Using tonal inflection to underscore and emphasize the intense sexual motion represented by the word "ridin."]

ED: She look like she foreal. [Stress on "real."]

BE: That's why I think she got paid, though. She ri: din. [Tonal emphasis.] Yeah, the whole video, she was workin like foreal. [Stress on "real."]

I think it is important to note too that ED, ET, and BE still see the women in the video as very feminine in their freestyled sex acts, although it could be said that the women in the video acted in ways that are gendered masculine. Rather than seeing the video women as degraded victims, the young ladies see them as workers who are trying to get paid, "workin like foreal," underscoring the value of entrepreneurship in Hiphop culture and the bottom-dollar logic of capitalist America. Not only do the girls reconstruct the gender roles of the women as represented in the video (and men) from the point of view of Hiphop ideology; they also read these roles against dominant racist discourse. In other words, the hiphoppas in the video represent people who have invented lives for themselves, made a way outa no way and are respected for so doing. From the point of view of dominant discourse, however, they are degraded, lesser forms of man- and womanhood. Both discourses, however, are embodied, Hiphop and dominant, as is apparent in the next example.

In Example Four, ED insists that the stripper video be interpreted as representing only some women—"Some women are and some women ain't. But, the way they was puttin it, was like, females." She underscores this point again with "It is some tip drills out here. It is. But then again, it ain't some."

Example Four

BE: Why you say it's degrading?

ED: Because. Foreal. You just don't. You ain't got to say all that. Know what Uhm saying? Like you said. Some women are and some women ain't. But, the way they was puttin it, was, like, females. Point blank. Period. That's in that song, females. Generalizing just all the females like that. But, know what Uhm sayin, you're right. It is some tip drills out here. It is. But then again, it ain't some.

BE: That's true.

ET: Well, a lot of the lyrics in the song is degrading to women. For instance, it said, "It must be yo ass cause it ain't yo face." He said, "It ain't no fun unless we all get some." You know what Uhm saying, so? Basically, meaning we gone run a train on you.

BE: But that's not degrading if the girls is wit it. It's some girls who wit dat. I don't think it's degrading. It's girls who is like that and they down for the git down, just how the boys is. Know what Uhm saying. I don't. I don't know.

Example Four also demonstrates the girls' questioning of the ways in which gender roles are ordered in the space of the strip club and by extension the staged strip club video. BE constructs women as free agents. She does not accept that the women are passive victims of males' sex drives as ET interprets the song's lyrics "It ain't no fun unless we all get some" to mean "[they] gone run a train on *you*." Rather, BE chimes in with "It's some girls who wit dat. I don't think it's degrading. *It's girls who is like that and they down for the git down, just how the boys is.* Know what Uhm saying." Underlying this utterance is the idea that it is just as natural for the girls to have group sex and not only to do it to please the males. On the other hand, what seems to trouble ED and ET is the fact that every Black female is a potential tip drill, and if this is the case a tip drill likes what she does and doesn't mind having a train run on her. BE is focusing on the strippers' agency, their control of sex acts. The conflicting language that ED and BE exhibit is influenced by their knowledge that the Black girls in the video are devalued, by virtue of the haunting controlling stereotypes imputed to all Black females since slavery.

In Example Five their knowledge of these stereotypes is fully unloaded. They use ample language that seeks to deconstruct several racist Black stereotypes.

Example Five

ER: Do you think that uhm, uhm, like, people who watch these videos that maybe don't know any, don't have any Black friends, do you think that that makes them think that this is how Black people act?

ET: To some extent yes, to some extent no.

BE: I think so.

ER: You do?

BE: I think that people think that Black women don't have respect for they self as much as other women do.

ER: Really?

BE: I mean if you just look at the way we're portrayed on TV. Either [three-second pause]. Know what Uhm saying. We poor. Ah mean it ain't nothin wrong wit being poor but Ahm just sayin, either we po-or, or we got fi-hunned [five hundred] kids.

ET: Yep. Kids. [Tonal agreement from both—overlap on "kI: dz."]

BE: No baby father. Our baby father in jail. We strippin. We naked on TV.

ET: Uhm hmm.

BE: Or we dancin. It's never like . . . I don't know.

ED: They never portray anything good. Just like . . . On the way comin up to State College we saw a billboard. And the billboard was talkin about don't, basically sayin not to drop out of school.

BE: It said, "Break the cycle."

ED: Yeah, it said "Break the cycle," don't drop outta school. But then it was talkin bout being pregnant. And then they had a big Black girl. I never see Black people on billboards, but for this one, I saw a Black girl on the billboard.

ER: Uhm . . . You gotta be kiddin. Sto: p.

BE: I could see if this was a community, where they was catering to the Black people, like for us, in our community. That's a message. Cause really, yeah, you need to break the cycle. Really.

ED: Right. Exactly.

ER: Right, right, right. This a White community.

BE: But this a White community. You see a Black person up there. What that mean?

ED: Every time they go pass the billboard, the only thing they gone think: Yeah those Black people they only have . . .

BE: . . . a eighth-grade education and have eighteen babies. Yep, but I think that, I think that it's just music and know what Uhm sayin, and I think Nelly wouldn't really approach a girl he really like like that.

ER: Uh hmm.

ED: Right.

BE: One who he thought was class, a girl who he really wanted to talk to, a girl he really wanted to talk to, he wouldn't say, "It ain't no fun if the homies can't have none."

ER: Uhm hmm, uhm hmm.

BE: Certain girls, niggas know they can do that wit.

ET: Certain girls is jump offs, and certain girls is wifeys.

One of the most obvious stereotypes from the point of view of the girls is that of the poverty-stricken, irresponsible breeding Black woman. As BE states: "look at the way we're portrayed on TV. Either [three second pause] . . . We poor. Ah mean it ain't nothin wrong wit being po-or but . . . either we poor, or we got fi-hunned kids." The conversation becomes communal here. The call–response and overlap in speech on the vocalization of the word [kI: dz] implies that this narrative is ubiquitous. Globalized technologies have spread this message far and wide. BE continues: "No baby father. Our baby father in jail. We strippin. We naked on TV." ED introduces into this narrative the billboard in a White community exploiting a "big Black girl" as the symbol of irresponsible childbirth. ED: "Yeah, it said, "Break the cycle," don't drop outta school. But then it was talkin bout being pregnant. And then they had a big Black girl." Knowing where ED's conversation is going, BE reveals: "I could see if this was a community, where they was catering to the Black people, like for us, in our community. That's a message. Cause really, yeah, you need to break the cycle. Really . . . But this a White community. You see a Black person up there. What that mean?" The young women see the billboard as spreading and recycling stereotypes to a remote White community—people who don't have meaningful contact with Black people—who will perhaps get to know Black people only through White social constructions of Blackness and popular media such as music videos. On the billboard the image of the Black pregnant adolescent mother represents worthlessness, a strain on the economy, an unproductive body. This is in contrast to the women portrayed in the video and in the strip club, both entities of the capitalist state. These women are not represented as homemakers or mothers; they are breadwinners, which transforms their worth as women. The only thing they breed is cash, at least as represented in the technology. But these women, at least potentially, are also homemakers and mothers, trying to make a life and a living in a market-driven society. After all, the occupation of stripping or even video model is a dead-end job. It is a youth-oriented job where age is devalued, thus a short-term occupation. ED, BE, and ET enact Black discourse that reflects and resists Black knowledge of the social world. In other words, the girls contest these stereotypes of Black life, revealing these stereotypes as mere profitable constructed commodities, not authentic Black cultural constructions. At the same time, though, they succumb to these stereotypes, as is evident in BE's and ET's statements:

BE: Certain girls, niggas know they can do that wit.
ET: Certain girls is jump offs, and certain girls is wifeys.

A study of sexuality conducted by Motivational Educational Entertainment, reported by Thulani Davis in the *Village Voice*, found similar anti-Black female attitudes. Researchers found fifteen negative terms used for Black women. Davis (2004) quotes one of the study's scholars, Beth Richie, as saying, "Young people today in lower-income black communities are facing a . . . whole set of stereotypical images of themselves—hypersexual, sexually irresponsible, not concerned with ongoing intimate relationships. [They] can't help but be influenced by those images." I would add that these stereotypes hover over all segments of the Black community, not just low-income Blacks, as is shown in my "rap session" discussion with BE, ED, and ET, who are all middle class. I concede, however, that lower-income Blacks may be more susceptible to these stereotypes.

Major factors in the discourse practices of African American males and females are racial oppression, the tension between dominant and vernacular social constructions associated with Black woman- and manhood, and the differential patterns of labor and gender roles. As with any cultural group, class, geographical location, and belief systems are also factors in African American male and female gender and discourse practices. The cultural past or African past of American Africans also influences their discourse and communication patterns. AAV theorists conceptualize vernacularity as the guiding impetus for the epistemological development of African American literacies, discourses, and rhetorics. Scholars have identified distinctive Black discourse patterns stemming from Black ways of knowing and interacting, wherein Black language users draw on this tradition yet adapt it to their rhetorical situations. (Smitherman, 1977/1986; Gates, 1988) An aspect of this system of Black creativity is a response to absence and desire, which can often be traced (in part) to an "economics of slavery." (Baker, 1984) The contemporary economic framework for Black narrative creation involves late capitalism, wherein dominant culture contributes to and celebrates highly marketable constructions of Blackness. The effect of these stereotypes is harmful to many African Americans but even more damaging to lower-income Black people as they are often in less insulated environments.

As can be gathered from this brief sketch, young people are able to "read the word in relation to the world" (in the words of Paulo Freire), or (as put by Sojourner Truth) they are able to "read men and nations" in some cases, such as the girls' reading of the billboard, or their contestation of the gendered labor of the women in the videos. However, our youth get mixed messages from most of the society's media about their racial, sexual, and gender identities. Our critical pedagogies must guide students beyond challenging to changing of systems that tolerate inequality, sexism, and racism. As educators, adults, parents, community activists, and caring human beings we must be more proactive about getting feminist education into our homes, our schools, and communities. This education pertains not only to adolescent females and their women elders but also to males. In this urgent age, stage, and phase of capitalism, sexism, and patriarchy, male scholar-activists such as Mark Anthony Neal are advocating to males of all ages that it is okay to be a Black heterosexual male and a feminist.[6] Neal asserts that one of the main issues that individuals who take this stand must face is being perceived as queer, thus men or women who work to heighten males' feminist consciousness must be aware of this and give young men strategies to deal with the issue. Neal (2005) is doing groundbreaking work around what it means to be a man and rethinking Black masculinity. In his work, he pushes what it means for men to expand their emotional range, learn how to nurture and do feminist politics as men.

In the next chapter, I continue to examine the relationship between controlling myths of Black womanhood and the language and literacy practices Black femalehiphoppas use to combat them, through my analysis of the Kimberly Jones perjury trial.

4

RIDE OR DIE B, JEZEBEL, LIL' KIM OR KIMBERLY JONES AND AFRICAN AMERICAN WOMEN'S LANGUAGE AND LITERACY PRACTICES

The naked truf

Since female rappers are *only entertainers*, should their language, literacy, and rhetorical practices be seriously considered? The topic brings several issues to the fore. Speaking of rap and African American discourse tradition in the same breath trivializes the historic and ongoing Black freedom struggle, doesn't it? Linking rap and Hiphop discourse to African American discourse conflates African American culture and street culture, don't it? There's no real culture to study in rap music for mass consumption, since rap has long become a global industry removed from its primary audience, right? And the global dominance of rap music and Hiphop culture is all about manhood in the new millennium, ain't it? Briefly, the answers to these questions are no, no, no, and no.

Now it is common knowledge that while Black culture and discourse are hybrid, so is American culture at large. A further aspect of this hybridity involves the impact of technologies on the interaction of discourses, between audience, speaker/performer, and the making of meaning. Paying Black folks and allowing us to participate in capitalist exploitation in no way solves the problem of valuing humanity equally. So examining the situation of African American female (and male) Hiphoppas offers a certain view of the struggle. We are still ravaged—if not physically, then psychologically—trying to figure out how to be whole persons when we are still three-fifths, if not by law, then by lived racialized, gendered, classed, and embodied experience (whatever type of body we have). In other words, though Hiphop culture emerged at a time when youth had access to markets and feed media conglomerations, the struggle for the minds and hearts of the people is what is at stake. What is our vision for ourselves as humans? And what images do we have of each other? African American and Hiphop discourses explore these and other questions about the meaning of life in today's world.

African American discourses come from people of all walks of life, including people on the ground, because many African Americans have been in non-insulated communities where we had to walk through the alleys of the shadows of death. In saying this I do not mean to vulgarize African American discourse, but to underscore the relationship between streetlife discourse and that of Hiphop. At this point in the industry, the preponderance of music that gets distributed globally or that gets into the airwaves focuses on various and sundry street characters: ballers, hustlers, fiends, prostitutes, drug dealers, pimps, various black market entrepreneurs, etc.—those who make a living from a devalued or officially over-looked sector of the lifeworld.

Hiphop discourse, no matter how commodified or blaxploited, offers an interesting view of the human freedom struggle and the knowledge that people have about the world. Study of folk culture is not constrained to isolated groups untouched by contemporary postindustrial society. Folk are "the people who know," who have a special knowledge from their vantage point of the world, from their routine social experiences. From this perspective, any group can be a folk group, including college students, housewives, astronauts, corporate executives, janitors, White folks, poor White folks, Americans, assistant district attorneys, and even African American female rappers.

What do we know about the language and literacy practices of African American female rappers? What influences these practices? What do we know about Black women rappers?[1] Their participation in rap music and Hiphop culture is without question. What many do question is: why? Why do women participate in this male-dominant genre? And how do they navigate this male-dominant space where they are largely represented in narrow, stereotypical ways? Tricia Rose's work (1994b) demonstrates that women rappers are reluctant about critiquing their male peers in racially mixed public audiences. Why? Many attribute this to the code of the streets. That is part of it, but other historic experiences and cultural factors affect African American female rappers' rhetorical practices. Gwendolyn Pough (2004) explains several rhetorical traditions that African American female rappers share with their female freedom-fighting ancestors. Linking the discourse practices of rappers such as Lil' Kim to female freedom fighters seems to be a bit of a stretch, but the lyrics below give us a hint:

> Spread love that's what a real mob do
> Keep it gangsta look out for your people (For your people)
> I'm the wicked bitch of the east, you better keep the peace (Aiyyo!)
> Or out come the beast
> We the best still there's room for improvement
> Our presence is felt like the Black Panther Movement
> (Lil' Kim, "The Jump Off")

Lil' Kim calls herself "the wicked bitch of the east" and alludes to the fact that she can be a "beast," simultaneously claiming that her presence is felt like the Black Panther Movement, inadvertently aligning herself with the likes of Elaine Brown, Kathleen Cleaver, and Angela Davis. Unlike their overtly political grandmothers who sought to redefine society, rappers, both male and female, largely seek to define a specific group in society. (See Bynoe, 1994.) Michael Dyson (2001: 153) asks the question: "Isn't the self—and not just one's public persona, even a thug one—an artistic creation? Can't it draw from the realm of collective experience embodied in cultural myths, racial allegories, and ghetto legends?" It is a provocative question that should be kept in mind as we explore the complex of "cultural myths," "racial allegories," and "ghetto legends" that informs the identity negotiations and discourse practices of Kimberly Jones/Lil' Kim and puts her at odds with the dominant Anglo-American discourse of the "United States of America" in the perjury trial, the United States of America vs. Kimberly Jones and Monique Dopwell.

Although Kimberly Jones's case is theoretically about perjury, it is also about racism, sexual exploitation, and gender oppression in the larger society and in Hiphop. This chapter focuses on the myth of the immoral Black Jezebel in American society, the prosecution's subtle employment of it to vilify Jones, and the language and literacy traditions upon which Jones drew to combat them. My thesis is that both Jones as a Black female and Lil' Kim the Queen Bee were tried and found to be immoral liars. Before getting into the nitty-gritty of Kim's language and literacy practices, we will begin by looking at the subtle ways in which the prosecution drew upon the myth of the immoral Black woman in their framing of the case.

The assistant district attorneys argued that as eyewitnesses, Kimberly Jones and Monique Dopwell (Kim's assistant) lied to the grand jury by stating that one of their colleagues, who was later found guilty, was not present at a shootout outside of a New York radio station. When shown a picture of another suspected shooter and colleague, Jones did not make a positive identification. The jury later found both Jones and Dopwell guilty of three counts of perjury and one count of conspiracy while acquitting them of an obstruction of justice charge. They were sentenced to 366 days in prison. Jones was also fined fifty thousand dollars.

Black women and the myth of Jezebel

It is historical fact that one of the myths that control the image of African American women is our supposed immorality. The battle for Kimberly Jones was all uphill not only because of her rap persona as Lil' Kim the Jezebel or wicked bitch, but from the historical stereotypes foisted onto enslaved African women who were thought to be immoral and "less deserving of protection from violence and sexual exploitation." (Yarborough and Bennett, 2000: 635) Jezebel is the bad Black female who is promiscuous, the embodiment of lust. She uses her sexually alluring nature and lewdness to entrap men and she can never be sexually exhausted, chaste, or truthful. Jezebel uses men who have something of value to offer. She's a golddigger.

> [As this relates to] African American women, [they] were not, and often are not, portrayed as being truthful and, therefore, they [cannot] be trusted. Throughout history, our court system has also exploited the myth

of Jezebel. The courts have used this image to make racism and sexism appear natural. The sexual myth of Jezebel functions as a tool for controlling African American women. Consequently, sexual promiscuity is imputed to them even absent specific evidence of their individual sexual histories. This imputation ensures that their credibility is doubted when any issue of sexual exploitation is involved.

(Yarborough and Bennett, 2000: 638)

The myth of the strong Black independent woman is also a socializing construct of Black womanhood. Historically, the Black woman has been socialized to be the backbone of Afro-American culture. Thus, the sociocultural orientation of Black women overwhelmingly teaches us to protect, serve, love, and nurture. During enslavement loved ones could be sold away and even oneself placed into new and dangerous situations at the discretion of enslavers in the blink of an eye. Even today, many Black mothers, daughters and sisters are in environments that are not constructed to insulate them. Further, Black men have been stereotyped as deviant. Thus, they too are subordinated in society. From a White supremacist patriarchal perspective, we don't feel it; and even if we do, we can handle it. Myths of gender and sexual inequality permeate the hidden transcripts or subtexts of society. A man's honor has historically been linked to his word, his need to right the wrongs done to his family. On the other hand, a woman's honor has always been connected to her purity—her virginity, chastity, or fidelity. Add to this "The negative images and myths created during slavery that justified the forced exposure of African American women's bodies to public inspection [that] still influence the customs, beliefs, and consequently, the law's treatment of African American women today." (Tribett-Williams, 2000: 171) As Yarbrough and Bennett (2000: 626) write: "[W]hen powerful institutions' or individuals' claims are juxtaposed against those of less powerful or powerless institutions and individuals, the attachment of credibility to the powerful itself becomes an indicia of power." In the eyes of the United States government, Kimberly Jones is powerless. She's an African American of humble beginnings, reared in the ghettoes of Brooklyn, New York; and, worse, she is a Black woman. She suffers from the colonized mentality pervasive in Black communities that values light skin and "good hair" (Caucasian features). Because of her parents' breakup, she, along with her mother, lived from hand to mouth, until she moved back home with her father, at which time his rules and behavior became unbearable, causing her to turn to a life of tricking, dating drug dealers, and participating in streetlife activities to survive. (Pough, 2004) Until she met Christopher Wallace, a.k.a. Biggie, a.k.a. the Notorious B.I.G., whom she grew to love deeply. He mentored her, and aided her in her dream to become a rap star, but they shared an Ike and Tina Turner type of relationship. Biggie abused, lied to, and cheated on Kim. Her lover's death further traumatized her. All of this occurred in her youth. Needless to say, the sista has come up the rough side of the mountain.

On the other hand, whether you like or dislike her music and her persona, Lil' Kim represents a type of power. She is the queen of the streets, the Queen Bitch, the Queen Bee, the Black Madonna of rap music. She is an overcomer. She is a global fashion icon. Lil' Kim's violation of sexual mores is threatening to some. As Imani Perry has eloquently argued (2004: 162), through their personas, among other vehicles, Black female rappers assert nationalism, articulate violence as opposed to victimization, express rage, frustration, instability, and insanity. In this way, female violence in Hiphop can be read beyond mere negativity and as a type of "hip hop feminist symbolism." Given this unacceptable representation of power coupled with financial success, it is no wonder that the government put Lil' Kim "in her place."

Jezebel on trial

The prosecutors used certain, mostly indirect, tactics that drew on the myth of the immoral Black woman, effectively conflating Lil' Kim, the Jezebel, with Kimberly Jones, the young Black woman on trial. The prosecutors on behalf of the grand jury questioned Jones two years and four months after the shootout that occurred in February 2001. Not long after the incident, the police uncovered a videotape placing Damion (D-Roc) Butler at the scene. A year and seven months before Jones was questioned, Butler had already confessed that he was present at the shootout. Further, witnesses for the prosecution, members of Lil' Kim's crew, testified that Suif Jackson (a.k.a. C. Gutta or Gutta) was there and revealed Kim's acquaintance with both men. Nevertheless, the prosecutors used Lil' Kim's video "No Matter What They Say" to demonstrate to the trial jury that she knew Jackson, as he appears in that particular video. In other words, they wanted to solidify in the minds of the jury that Jones is a liar based on the video. This bit of evidence probably wouldn't raise an eyebrow if the performance was within the approved limits of Black girl behavior. In the video, Lil' Kim is featured in various sexually revealing outfits that show off her lovely young body with various suggestive dance moves, including grabbing her crotch. In several scenes, she is in sexually suggestive positions, lying on a couch, or sitting in a chair with her legs spread open. The Jezebel imagery is clear. Lil' Kim, the temptress, is in total control of her surroundings and the people in them. She is the center of attention of all males and females in the video, as though she is THEE person to know. She gets what she wants and knows how to get it—by hook or by crook. The song's lyrics and the video imagery work in concert to enforce the theme. Within her performance of "No Matter What They Say," Lil' Kim performs several attributes of the Black Jezebel. She clearly refers to golddigging, manipulating and exploiting many men, and asserts no concern for what others think about it. The prosecution had already secured numerous documents and photos from Jones' offices showing that these men worked for her, had vacationed with her, went on tour with her. Did they really need to show this music video? Could any jurist honestly separate Lil' Kim's rap persona from Kimberly Jones, the woman on trial?

While being investigated by the grand jury, the prosecutors asked Kim to interpret for them a song on her *Notorious K.I.M* CD wherein she pretends to be a

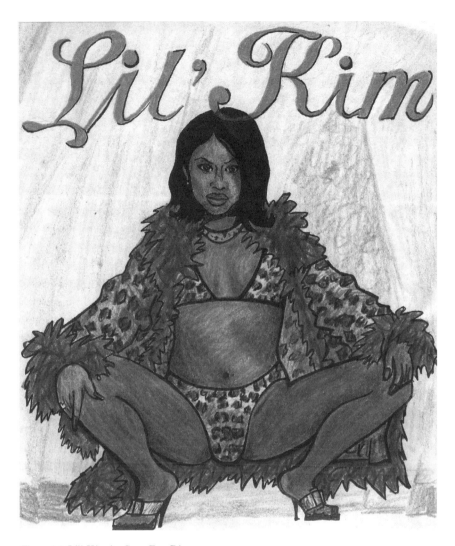

Figure 4.1 Lil' Kim by Sara Eve-Rivera

defendant on trial for the murder of six law-enforcement officers. To this query, Kim replies: "If you don't know our music, you can really misinterpret it."[2] Below is a brief extract of the piece:

> [Pretend bailiff:] Will the court please rise, Judge Fuck Dr. Spock residing.

> [Pretend prosecuting attorney:] Your Honor, Little Kim is a threat to society. She has shown a blatant disregard for the law and has killed six

fine law-enforcement agents in the line of duty. For these vicious acts, she should be punished to the fullest extent of the law.

[Lil' Kim:] Pardon me, Your Honor, may I address the bench?
They tryin to assassinate me like they did to Larry Flint
Uhm uhm, excuse my persona
I may be hardcore, but I'm not Jeffrey Dahmer
Ever since I killed 'em, I ain't been in trouble since
Wasn't my fault, I acted out of self-defense
He killed my best friend

[Pretend Prosecuting Attorney]: Who is him?

[Lil'Kim]: I mean them
They was all dressed in blue and they want me dead too
They had real grenade bombs inside of they palms
And a whole bunch of guns wrapped tight in they arms
See them bastards woke me up when they broke my alarm
I was gittin my ass licked by this cat name Tom
(Lil' Kim, "Lil' Drummer Boy," *Notorious K.I.M.*, 2000)[3]

Further, the prosecution also used liner notes from Lil' Kim's CDs *Hardcore* and *Notorius K.I.M.* They already knew from their witnesses the significance of shoutouts in Hiphop ideology, that shoutouts are ritual forms of verbal respect paid to members of someone's crew or to significant people, based on childhood or family ties, or a certain style that the artist must acknowledge. (See Morgan, 2001.) They also knew that Suif Jackson's nickname was C. Gutta and Damion Butler's was D-Roc. Lil' Kim's liner notes on *Hardcore* said: "To my mothafuckin crew, Lil'Ceasar . . . Big brother Dee Rockafella [D-Roc], C Gutta." Lil' Kim's shoutouts on the *Notorious K.I.M.* CD were: "Gutta, Gutta . . . thanks for holding me down. I love you all." It is well known that Hiphop has been criminalized, and, of the various "commonsense" reasons for this indictment, one is Hiphoppas' organization on the mafia family model. In Lil' Kim's case, it probably hurt her more because she was the first lady of a crew called "Jr. Mafia." However, this model was exploited for purposes of organized rhyme, not organized crime. Again, the Lil' Kim image of immorality is indirectly drawn upon to crush Kimberly Jones' credibility.

During the grand jury investigation, it became apparent that in 1996 Kimberly Jones had been arrested while visiting at her then boyfriend Christopher "Biggie" Wallace's home; so was Suif Jackson, though their arrests were at different times, they weren't in the house together, and Kim was released from any wrongdoing. Prosecutor Cathy Seibel states during summation that Kimberly Jones was sleeping in Biggie's bed when the police arrived, and that she had a "bunch of cash lying around," which proves that she was there regularly. Further, Suif Jackson also used Biggie's address as his own. One of the reasons why Seibel gives these details is to show that Jones knew Jackson. On the surface, this is normal fact-finding on the part of investigators. However, one cannot overlook the fact that the picture painted of Kimberly Jones is of her being in the bed with a large amount of cash. Again, the implication here is that she's immoral.

Another aspect of the myth of the immoral woman is that she is opportunistic and manipulative. She uses men and then dumps them when they can no longer fulfill her desires financially or otherwise. The prosecution drew on this facet of the myth in at least two ways. They accused Kim of not really caring about her lover, Biggie's death, stating that if she really cared she would enquire about and search out his murderers. The implication here is that Biggie had served his purpose in her life by mentoring her and creating an opportunity for her to become Lil' Kim, the platinum-selling recording artist.

Similarly, the prosecution produced witnesses, James Lloyd, a.k.a. Lil' Cease, and Antoine Spain, a.k.a. Banga, who revealed an alleged romantic relationship between Kimberly Jones and Damion Butler. This sends a message that Kim sexually exploited Butler and dropped him when she no longer needed his services. The prosecution used these statements to show that Kim may have had an ulterior motive for dumping Butler. Lil' Cease and Banga testified that Kim and Damion had a boyfriend/girlfriend relationship and that they had had a huge fight, with Butler throwing Jones out of a house in Leonia. Testimony of this relationship, not only implies that Kim is a woman scorned but adds one more man to the chain of Kim's sexual partners. In fact, Kim's attorney, Mel Sachs, has her testify directly to the allegation of a sexual relationship:

Sachs: Now, did you have a sexual relationship with Damion Butler?
Jones: No. Everyone speculated.
Sachs: When you say speculated, what do you mean by that?
Jones: Well, everyone speculated. When Puffy was managing me they all spec-
        ulated that I was sleeping with him, too.
Sachs: And the relationship with Damion Butler was what? How would you—
Jones: We were close. You know, we were cool. Him and Biggie were friends. Him
        and I developed a friendship from there. And, you know, it was basically
        management.[4]

Jones' answers show the plight of women in the uninsulated world of business. It is always assumed that the only talent a women needs to succeed is sexual availability to male colleagues—the old casting couch. However, Kim goes on to explain why she had to relieve Butler from co-managing her career. He fought on a video shoot that was important to Kim's career, he allegedly had Antoine Spain beaten in Kim's home, and he stole Kim's jewelry. Mel Sachs stresses repeatedly that Kim had severed all ties with Damion Butler. His intention in highlighting this is to show Kim's distance from criminal activities or active criminals and that she didn't orchestrate the shootout. She too was a victim who was traumatized by the shootout and several other altercations. The prosecution uses Kim's separation from Butler, however, to show that she is an opportunist. Cathy Seibel says:

[I]t's hardly surprising that Kimberly Jones would want to protect Damion Butler, even though he and she had gone their separate ways. It's hardly surprising to why she might want to do that for him, and . . . for herself.

. . . Kimberly Jones' records and Capone's got banned from Hot 97 . . . If you're a rapper not getting your spins, not getting your records played on Hot 97 can drive down your sales and hurt your career and your pocketbook.

. . . Now lucky for her, her second album, *Notorious K.I.M.*, had been released back in June of 2000, so the period where her singles were [not] getting a lot of airplay was over . . . [T]hat's when she's promoting her third album, *La Bella Mafia*. The last thing she wants is for that can of worms to be opened up again. The last thing she wants is for the grand jury's investigation to reveal that two of her entourage were on that sidewalk shooting. That wouldn't be good for business.[5]

At the end of the day, though, if beefs produce hit records, regardless of airplay, word of a record's hotness spreads through the hoods, suburbs, and the World Wide Web like fire and actually fuels record sales.[6] Dissing on record can boost an artist's career if well done. Even more importantly, record companies benefit greatly at the risk of artists' safety as these diss records can end in someone's death. It is well known that Lil' Kim and Foxy Brown had beef. Both female artists had records dissin the other. Many listeners may have interpreted Lil' Kim's "This is a Warning" on *La Bella Mafia* as a diss to Foxy, as Kim makes several threats (though not addressed to any one particular person) throughout the song. And there are other songs on *La Bella Mafia* that contain lyrics that some listeners may interpret as directed at Foxy, though Foxy's name is mentioned only once on the album. "Get in Touch with Us," for example, contains lyrics that some listeners may consider violent. In any case, the record that is alleged to be at the center of the shootout is the one on which Foxy dissed Lil' Kim: Capone N. Noreaga's "Bang Bang." When Capone arrived at Hot 97 for his interview on the same day as the station's interview with Lil' Kim all hell broke loose. Though the grand jury's investigation revealed that Lil' Kim had no part in the shooting itself, the indirect implication is that Kim is at the center of the shootout, or at least both Kim and Foxy Brown are the cause of it, as they are both immoral Black Jezebels, if only in image, which was obviously enough for the grand jury to indict Kim.

Kimberly Jones and African American female literacies

Repeatedly both the prosecution and the defense appealed to the jury to employ their "common sense." The foregoing discussion exemplifies the "commonsense" notions and myths that undergird our society when it comes to women, and Black women in particular. You know if the United States Senate attacked the integrity of Law Professor Anita Hill, a paragon of virtue, Lil' Kim didn't stand a chance. (See Smitherman, 1987/2000: 251–67.)

Figure 4.2 Lil' Kim and Foxy Brown by Sara-Eve Rivera

Knowledge of African American female literacies informs the framework necessary to an understanding of the discourse practices surrounding the Kimberly Jones case. In an earlier work (Richardson, 2003), I argued that the concept of African American female literacies refers to ways of knowing and acting and the development of skills, vernacular expressive arts and crafts that help females to advance and protect themselves and their loved ones in society. African cultural traditions—such as spirituality or humor, for example—that are constantly adapted to meet the needs of navigating life in a racist society influence these practices and ways of knowing and coping. To a degree greater than that of many Anglo American males and females, we are socialized to realize ourselves as racial and sexual objects and as the embodiment of immorality. These interlocking aspects of our multiple consciousnesses play a significant role in the development of African American female language and literacy practices. The Black woman's conscious-ness of her condition/ing, her position/ing in society, and the condition/ing of her audiences must be factored into analysis of language use. African American females communicate their literacies through storytelling, conscious manipulation of silence and speech, code/style shifting, and signifying, among other verbal and non-verbal practices.

Prosecutors asked Kimberly Jones 2,367 questions over five days during the grand jury investigation. The prosecutors convinced the jury that her answers to two of those questions—Was Damion Butler present? Do you know Suif Jackson?—were false. However clear this may seem on the surface, when we look at the circumstances surrounding the case, the prosecutors' actual questions, and Jones' responses, the situation is more complex. Jones is operating within the dictates of African American and Hiphop discourse, while the prosecutors are operating out of dominating White Anglo-American legal discourse.

The strong Black woman doing verbal battle

Kim's lawyer called her to testify on March 10, 2005. His strategy had been to show the court and the jury the true Kimberly Jones rather than the image Lil' Kim. What better way for the court to see this than through Kim's telling of her life story? Storytelling remains one of the most powerful language and literacy practices that Black women use to convey their special knowledge.

Sachs: And before you became an entertainer, could you please tell the members of the jury the jobs that you had?

Kim: Well, I worked at H&R Block, I worked at a bank, I was a transfer agent. I also worked at Bloomingdale's. Those were the main jobs that I had . . .

Sachs: And could you tell the members of the jury about your upbringing, your early years?

Kim: Well, *I didn't exactly have a great life*. My mom and my dad split when I was maybe ten years old, and I end up going with my mom. And my dad came back and fought for me because me and my dad was really close, but I was also close with my mom, so *that was tough for me*. And when my dad came back and fought for me, we had to go to court, my dad won, and I remember my mom being really sad.

And during that time *my dad and I started going through a lot, and I ran away from home*. And I remember like I didn't know exactly where my mom was at the time, but I heard she was living in the Bronx, so I kind of tracked her down then I started staying with her. But *I loved my dad and I loved my mom, so I was just going through a lot*.

At the time my mom started going through a lot. She really wasn't working, I was staying with my mom. We ended up living out of—basically out of the trunk of her car . . . My dad got remarried, and ever since then I kind of been on my own. So I started living back with my mom because I wanted to live with my dad because I just loved to go with him and I *didn't know where I wanted to be, but I ended up going back and forth* . . .

Sachs: Now tell me, how did you become a performer?

Kim: Well, around the time when I was working, *I think at the time I had two jobs*. I think I was working at H&R Block and Bloomingdale's. I was coming home because I was, like I said, at one point I would go back and forth between my mom and my dad, and I think this was around the time that I was going to see my dad and I was working at Bloomingdale's. *I remember I had on high heels, even back then, I was probably fourteen years old, fifteen, I don't know, and I had on high heels, I had a knapsack on my back because I was coming from Bloomingdale's, that was my second job that I had at night,* and I saw the Notorious B.I.G. sitting on a garbage can. And he said to me: "I heard you know how to rap."

... Then he was like "Let me hear something." To put it plain and simple, put a long story short, I started learning rapping from him and I was with Biggie ever since.[7]

Kim's use of language works to humanize herself in the eyes of the jury and construct an image of herself as simultaneously an ordinary girl and a girl whose life has been marked for extraordinary struggle. She's ordinary because she worked jobs like any person from the rank and file of society does. She had a father who was in the home, at least until her parents broke up. But like any child might be, the young Kim is torn because of this and her deep love for both her parents. Unlike most children, though, young Kim has to work two jobs—one at night. In high heels (she repeats for emphasis) at the age of fourteen or fifteen, she walks through the city with a knapsack on her back moving from one job to the next. Unsheltered Black girls, in order to survive and navigate their lives in this world, must know early that they are sexually and racially marked objects, to a degree greater than many White American boys or girls. Kim's "high heels" signify this knowledge.

Under her attorney's questioning, Kim goes on to discuss her role as philanthropist, the organizations she's sponsored, her work as a multifaceted artist with well-respected companies, products, and other stars. She names one of her charities Lil' Kim Cares. Then Mel Sachs gets to the crux of the case and affords Kim the opportunity to confront the public's "commonsense" notions about the bad Black girl when he asks:

Sachs: Now, let me ask you this. Is there a difference between the image of Lil' Kim and Kimberly Jones?

Kim: Of course, of course there is. I'm really nothing like my music, a lot of people say. You know, I'm proud of what I do. I love to do what I do, I'm an entertainer. Lil' Kim is the name that I use to just—is my image. Lil' Kim is my image. That's who I am when I'm rapping, when I'm a celebrity. Kimberly Jones, Kimberly Denise Jones, is who I am when I go home.[8]

Kim as nurturer, protector, and survivor is operative in the following exchange between Assistant District Attorney Cathy Seibel and Kimberly Jones:

Seibel: As a victim, you certainly wanted to be as helpful as you could in finding out who did this? [Referring to the shootout of February, 2001.]

Jones: At that time, I'm just thinking, you know, my family, my mother. I'm thinking about Mo's kids. I'm just thinking—a lot of times when traumatic moments happen in my life, I just shut down. I don't know how you would handle it, or anyone else, but I just shut down.

Seibel: As a victim, you certainly want the police investigation to be as successful as possible to try to find the people who victimized you, right?

Jones: I can't really answer that, because I'm the type of person, if something like
        that happens in my life and—as you know, if you're reading up on me,
        there has been a lot of things that happened in my life. I just shut down
        and keep on moving. I don't dwell on the past. A lot of things just can't be
        figured out, like Biggie's death. I just keep on moving. That was very
        traumatic for me.

(Reported in Matthews, 2005: 116)

Jones reveals that she did what she did for the sake of others—her family and "Mo"
and "Mo's kids." "Mo" refers to Kim's co-defendant, Monique Dopwell, her friend
who sometimes doubles as her assistant. Dopwell is a single mother who worked
for Best Buy, when she was not on tour with Kim. Kim's loyalty to her family and
friends who depend on her is a far cry from the insatiable Jezebel who is all about
her scrilla.[9] Asserting dominant culture's understanding of the relationship of police
to citizen, Seibel assumes that Kim shares in this worldview. But as an African
American woman, Kim knows that fraternizing with the NYPD, the LAPD, or any
of the folks in blue can be hazardous to one's health and in the long run still can't
fix "the things that happened in [her] life." Her strategy is just to "keep on moving."
Omitted from Kim's remarks are her thoughts about Damion and Suif, who were
also part of her extended family. Kim adheres not only to the code of the street but
to the code of many African American women. She adheres to secrecy and silence.
Some African American women, myself included, have been "programmed to
believe that racism always trumps sexism, and that the 'hierarchy of interests within
the Black community assigns a priority to protecting the entire community against
the assaultive forces of racism.'" (Yarborough and Bennett, 2000: 643) "Don't help
put a brother in jail." "Just move on with your life."

   Kim's role as protector and strong Black woman works in tandem with her use
of indirect language. In the summation of the case, Seibel reads Jones' grand jury
testimony to show "What really happened?"

Q: J3, who was that? [J3 refers to a picture featuring Suif Jackson.]
A: I don't *really* know him too *well.*
Q: Have you seen him before?
A: Not *really*. I don't know him *too well.*
Q: You don't recognize that person at all?
A: No.
Q: When you say you don't know him too well, do you know him a little bit?
A: *I think* I have seen him, but I don't know him *too well. I don't know his name.*
Q: Where do you think you have seen him?
A: I have seen him *around.* He has a *familiar* face.
Q: Has he ever been to your home?
A: No.
Q: Do you know who his friends are?
A: No.

Q: Do you recall when you saw him?
A: No.
A: Do you recall where you saw him?[10]

It is clear that the prosecutors want to hear Kimberly Jones corroborate that the person in the picture is Suif Jackson. But they never ask her if the person is Jackson, and Kim uses various indirect speech forms such as "really" and "well" which are said to be general features of women's language that African American women share with Anglo American women to hedge or demonstrate a less assertive tone. (See Troutman, 2001.) She never flat out says his name, or that she hasn't seen him. Other terms that add to the sense of ambiguity are "around" in "I've seen him around" and "familiar" in "He has a familiar face."

Seibel reads more of the grand jury transcript on this matter:

A: He is familiar. I don't know him, though.
Q: He looks familiar to you?
A: Yes.
Q: But you don't know his name? Do you know why he looks familiar to you?
A: He looks like he has been around in the industry before.
Q: When you say the industry, what do you mean?
A: The music industry, but I don't know him.[11]

Again, Kim's language, geared toward recognizing the photograph not the man in it, allows her the option of not having to know the name of the man in the photograph for sure.

The prosecution returns again to their earlier line of questioning:

Q: Who is J3?
A: I don't know him *that well*.
Q: You have never seen this person before?
A: *I think* I have seen [him] *around*, but I don't know him *that well*.[12]

Kimberly Jones continues to employ indirect speech so that the onus of interpretation is on the prosecutors. She does not directly state what they want to hear. The terms "that well," "I think," and "around," lend to the ambiguity of the message.

Aspects of Kim's worldview, of her culture's wisdom, are also revealed in her responses to Seibel in the closing statements, as in the following:

> Isn't he a friend of Damion Butler's? She says, "I don't know. Maybe that's where I have seen him." Then she is asked if the man in J3 has been around her? . . . She denies it. She says: "I haven't really seen him around. I think I might have seen him around in the industry. And if he's friends with Damion Butler, maybe that's why I have seen him." Then when she is asked if she has seen him many times before, she flatly says "no."[13]

According to defense attorney Mel Sachs in the opening statement, Kim is asked by the prosecutor: "Isn't it correct that you know that the person pictured in the photograph is a friend of Damion Butler's?" To this question, she answers: "*I don't know that*, maybe that's where I saw him around."[14]

Pertaining to the query about the person in the photograph being a friend of Damion Butler, the prosecutors want Jones to confirm that Suif Jackson is actually a shooter present in the altercation assisting Butler. But they do not directly ask Kim that. They ask if the person in the photograph is the friend of Butler. Some indirection and signifying is apparent in this answer. In the African American verbal tradition, signifying can be employed as "a sociolinguistic corrective employed to drive home a serious message without preaching or lecturing." (Smitherman, 1987/2000: 255) Thus, Kimberly's response, "I don't know that . . ." is appropriate and true. Why? Because in African American culture it is general knowledge that everybody who smiles in your face is not your friend. This is true of the man in the photograph and of all the Black men and women in her life. Kim's response invokes this truism however indirectly to a Black audience. Unsatisfied with her response, the prosecution asks her: "This man in this photograph has been around you; correct?" Her answer is: "I haven't seen him *around*. *I think I might* have seen him *around* in the industry. And *if he's friends with Damion Butler, maybe* that's why I have seen him."[15] The prosecutors use the tag question "correct?" to encourage Kim to respond in a short, affirmative way, but she offers indirect narrative snippets, which employ generalities and conditionals such as "around," "I might," "if he's friends with Damion," and "maybe."

Did Kimberly Jones lie to us?

What I hope to have demonstrated is that the myths and images that play a crucial role in the language and literacy practices of African American female rappers are the same ones that influence those of all Black women. Kimberly Denise Jones is *not* Jezebel and neither are we. She plays the role of Lil' Kim the Jezebel and this role is open to all women, especially Black women, who want to enjoy the so-called finer things of life, within or without working rank-and-file jobs. The Strong Black Woman and Jezebel are exploited by capitalist–patriarchal systems to justify the normalcy of society's treatment of Black women. Kimberly Jones rapped for Hiphop and Black culture, but at the same time, she became a victim of the stereotypical images that have historically exploited Black women. And that's the naked truf.

5

"YO MEIN RAP IS PHAT WIE DEINE MAMA"

African American language in online German Hiphop, or identifying the global in global Hiphop

Figure 5.1 Turkish-German rapper Eko Fresh by Sara-Eve Rivera

> The absorption of [African American Language] into Eurocentric culture masks its true origin and reason for being. It is a language born from a culture of struggle; a way of talking that has taken surviving African language elements as the base for the creation of self-expression in an alien tongue.
>
> (Smitherman, 1998: 216)

> Hip-hop and rap cannot be viewed simply as an expression of African American culture; it has become a vehicle for global youth affiliations and a tool for reworking local identity all over the world. Even as a universally recognized popular musical idiom, rap continues to provoke attention to local specificities. Rap and hip-hop outside the USA reveal the workings of popular music as a culture industry driven as much by local artists and their fans as by the demands of global capitalism and U.S. cultural domination.
>
> (Mitchell, 2001: 2)

These two epigraphs point to a longstanding conundrum in cultural studies—the appropriation of Black cultural forms by non-Black people. One reason for the perplexity surrounding Black cultural borrowing is the haunting stereotype of the inferiority of African ancestry. For Smitherman, when Black cultural forms such as African American Language cross over, the experiences of the creators of the form are sanitized, divorced from their painful yet resilient cultural context, or disunderstood. "Black cultural forms" is here taken to mean sociocultural practices forged from existing African ideologies and practices and those that people of Black African descent encountered, developed, and/or appropriated in the context of negotiating life in European-dominant societies. As Mitchell indicates: if Black folks originated Hiphop and rap and others take up these expressions, they are no longer *simply* African American.

Hiphoppas from around the globe enlist AAL to (re)construct, maintain, negotiate, and/or resist their local situations and identities. An often-overlooked point is that Black experiences have a complex universal dimension. African American influence is probably more extensive than is usually recognized in the globalization of languages and development of resistance ideologies. In his study of global Englishes, Japanese Hiphop, and performativity, Pennycook (2003: 523) argues that the study of global Englishes and "raplishes" must be contextualized within the current phase of imperialism, that is "Globalizing/Corporatizing design." Studying the uses of Englishes from this perspective captures "the relationship between the ways in which some languages are no longer tied to locality or community, but rather operate globally in conjunction with these other scapes"—mediascapes, ethnoscapes, technoscapes, financescapes, and ideoscapes. Pennycook demonstrates how a Japanese rap group used English to invent a new Japanese identity, reflecting a consciousness of how they may be seen from outside their locality. He writes (2003: 527):

> In a sense, then, this use of Japanese and English-Japanese which may locate these rappers as decidedly local (from Kinshichoo) or which may

signal their sense of cultural mixing, and English that at times explicitly echoes African American English while at other times seems more Japanese in its usage—seems to constantly pull back and forth, to flow itself across the boundaries of identity.

I suspect that a part of the identity that they are trying to project is the authentic Hiphoppa, which they index with Japanese but also with AAL. When I say authentic Hiphoppa, I do not mean these Hiphoppas are claiming Afro-American Blacknesses, but that in their performance of Hiphop they are simultaneously adopting certain key paradigmatic elements of Black performance cultures.

The present work explores the sociolinguistic consequences of the globalization of AAL and culture into other languages through Hiphop discourse practices, particularly as they appear in online German Hiphop. Before moving into analysis of Germanized AAL/Hiphop, I begin by giving brief background on German Hiphop.

German Hiphop offline and on

Bennett's (1999) work on Hiphop culture in Germany demonstrates that radio and TV programming for occupying U.S. soldiers brought popularity of American culture to Germans, so much so that when the soldiers officially left, the programming remained. Bennett (1999: 77) suggests that one strand of German Hiphop performance, as opposed to the mere consumption of it, is dominated by people of African descent, namely, people from North Africa; other major performers are Turkish immigrants. Bennett (1999: 81–2) offers important information for our consideration of language contact and borrowing of AAL:

> In Frankfurt and other German cities, an early attempt to develop hip-hop beyond its African-American context and rework it as a medium for the expression of local themes and issues came as a number of local rap groups began incorporating German lyrics into their music. On the surface, such a move could be seen as a logical progression from the point of view of a generation of young hip-hoppers for whom German, if not their mother tongue, had become their adopted tongue following many years of living in the country. In switching from English to German rapping, it could be argued, a new measure of accuracy was made possible between localized social experience and linguistic representation. In reality, however, German rap has been by no means universally accepted by hip-hop enthusiasts in Frankfurt.

German Hiphop began by imitation of African American rap and the experiences it conveyed, eventually incorporating local experiences and language. Though not identical to African American experiences of oppression, two similar themes of racism are apparent in the language/lyrics of Afro-Deutsch Hiphop groups: "fear and anger instilled by racism and the insecurity experienced by many young members of ethnic minority groups over issues of nationality." (Bennett, 1999: 83) One group representing this situation is Advanced Chemistry. This German rap group consists of three males of Italian, Ghanaian, and Haitian backgrounds. Because of the racial background of two of the members, one might expect that such a group would adopt certain concepts from AAL into their German Hiphop vernacular.[1] Pennay (2001: 121) identifies two other types of German Hiphop groups. One school of Hiphop in Germany considers itself traditional, meaning that rap should be practiced in conjunction with wider Hiphop—"breakdance, graffiti, freestyling and a code of honor." In their study of the 'Recontextualization of hip-hop in European Speech Communities' Androutsopoulos and Scholz (2002) report that in "Germany . . . only a small percentage of hip-hoppers belong to ethnic minorities (2nd/3rd generation migrants of Turkish, Italian, Greek, etc. origin). However, these are an integral part of local hip-hop scenes." More popular is the trend represented by the White, middle-class, conservative, German-language rap group Die Fantastischen Vier (The Fantastic Four), whose music, called lovers' rap, focuses on personal relationships and universal themes.[2]

Pennay (2001) explains that after a trip to the U.S. the group realized that it had nothing in common with U.S. rappers and changed its style to reflect their own realities. Though Die Fantastischen Vier is officially credited as the originators of German Hiphop, "[German] Hip Hop was created by interaction of different communities of color, creative reaction to the inner cities' increasing pauperisation—a trend, which in Europe, too, disproportionately affects migrants and communities of color." (El-Tayeb, 2003: 477) The Eastern European migrant group is the largest in Western Europe and migration patterns structure them in poorer areas. Though they are considered White and European, they too experience racialized discrimination in the West. The "visible Other," though, are the Africans, Arabs, and Turkish Muslims. (El-Tayeb, 2003: 486)

From this brief background sketch of German Hiphop, it is reasonable to guess that there will be some correlation between degree of social identification with African Americans and adoption of AAL/Hiphop language among German Hiphoppas.

55.3 percent of the German population over the age of fourteen is online and those between the ages of fourteen and nineteen (94.7 percent) constitute the largest population of users. (http://www.ard.de/intern/index_view.phtml?k2=4andk3=7 andk4=1) Though Morgan (2001) is referring to the American context, citing Wheeler, she argues that adolescents of both sexes between the ages of twelve and seventeen make up the core of Hiphop practitioners. They, more than other age groups, listen to, memorize, and write raps. This cohort approximates the profile of the majority of German Internet users. At the time of writing, the search term 'German Hiphop' in Yahoo Deutschland yielded 816,000 site matches. Though White German Hiphoppas probably have the largest online presence, the presence of racial and ethnic-minority German Hiphoppas should not be discounted.

The Internet has become an important site for human communication, offering visibility and communication for Hiphop practitioners who may be geographically or culturally removed from centers of origins or familiar routes. Hiphoppas have taken to the web and use it as a means of representing, preserving, critiquing, and controlling the images and issues of the culture. (Richardson and Lewis, 2000) One issue that arises with the digital flow of Hiphop across the globe is the internationalization and recontextualization of Hiphop discourse. The case in hand is German-speaking Hiphoppas' borrowing of AAL/Hiphop as demonstrated in their online written discourse. There are several generalizations that can be made about the language contact situation presented by representing AAL/Hiphop/ German online. First, the writers envision their audiences to be proficient in German and to have a level of Hiphop literacy, which includes a heightened consciousness of Hiphop orality. Second, in certain cyberspaces visuality and/or writing is the major or only means of communication. Other contextualization cues, such as intonation, rhythm, prosody, and body gestures, are not available to aid in meaning making—for example, in chat rooms, guestbooks, or bulletin boards. Although there is an infinite amount of meaning-making potential, some meanings are privileged over others as Hiphop communicators/writers may imagine their words to have sound and visual effects because of the audience's familiarity with various Hiphop forms. Thus, and third, the ideal readers must have intimate local (German) knowledge and proficient knowledge of core concepts of Hiphop as it is understood in the donor culture in order to understand the full probabilities of the semantic context. Fourth, in certain cyberspace writings, the racial and ethnic background of the writer (and reader) is unknown. In a sense, the cyber-environment frees up participants. The evaluation of one's authentic incorporation of AAL/Hiphop would be based on: "who the [writers] and recipients were, what their relationship was, the degree of their involvement with [Hiphop] culture, the particular occasion, the specific contours of the character being claimed and so forth." (Rampton, 1995: 279)[3] Equally important would be the writer's usage of the appropriate (in/formal) language conventions in cyber genres, for example, chat rooms, or bulletin boards. The data that I present below, arguably, represent German Hiphoppas' claim to authenticity through their use of Hiphop discourse.

Data analysis

To illustrate the interpretation of linguistic choices related to German Hiphoppas' adoption of AAL/Hiphop ideology, I will analyze examples of language borrowing between German and AAL/Hiphop. A research assistant who has spent some time in Berlin translated eighty-five pages. Content on these sites focused on American as well as German rap scenes. German rap lyrics and computer-mediated conversations were analyzed to observe Germans' production of AAL/Hiphop. The bulk of data came from several German-based Hiphop-related websites: rap.de, rheimland.de, Mzee.com, HipHopLyrics.de, TFGNK,[4] and Ksavas.de. I chose the websites for three reasons. First, as I worked on a project investigating the online presence of Hiphop in South Africa and African America in 1998 (Richardson and Lewis, 2000: 251–76), I became aware of the adoption of African American Hiphop language and literacy practices by Hiphoppas around the globe, and I began collecting tokens. Some of my favorite examples of German incorporation of AAL/Hiphop came from a rap.de guestbook in 1998–9 that is no longer available online. Therefore, I have supplemented those with current data from guestbooks at Mzee.com and rheimland.de. The guestbook conversations led me to check out a small sampling of lyrics of three German rappers: Eko Fresh, Kool Savas, and 808 Mafia. Second, the Internet provides virtual access to the world and an alternate means of studying communication. Third, as I am not proficient in German, the written format enabled me to see German/AAL Hiphop. Websites were analyzed for their use of AAL/Hiphop guided by Smitherman (2000), Morgan (2001) and (2002), and my own native-speaker competence as a member of several Afro-American speech communities. The language samples have not been edited.[5] Approximately four hundred AAL/Hiphop words or phrases have been gleaned, counted as tokens, and divided into different categories commonly identified with codeswitching, language borrowing, or language crossing.

I do not claim that all of the terms are new borrowings into German because of Hiphop, as jazz, blues, and soul have long reached Germany. However, the German Hiphop generation is perhaps acquiring their AAL from their participation in Hiphop. I am interested in both the linguistic processes revealed in German Hiphoppas' use of AAL/Hiphop and the social implications of the language usage. To document the grammatical incorporation of AAL/Hiphop into German, for the most part, I rely upon Matrix Language Frame (MLF) theory, as developed by Myers-Scotton (2002) to support my analysis–content morpheme, code mixing, embedded language (EL). I also identify calques. To illustrate broader interpretation of linguistic choices, I rely on Marcyliena Morgan's (2001) discussion of Hiphop's language ideology, Smitherman (2000: 268–83), and H. Samy Alim's (2004) concept of "Hiphop Nation Language." From this point of view, German Hiphoppas' use of Hiphop language and literacy practices indexes their identities as authentic practitioners of Hiphop's elements. I close by speculating upon the implications this has for "Global Hiphop."

What it be? Hiphop's ideology

Morgan's (2001: 193) definition of Hiphop language ideology provides a framework for analysis of Germanized AAL/Hiphop. In Hiphop language ideology, the crew is the significant speech community unit. Crews can be neighborhood based, and are often founded on an extended family model, wherein members are expected to be loyal, support, and "represent" each other. Each crew has a particular style, local knowledge, and common knowledge about wider popular culture. Knowledge of vernacular, standard, and general language is essential so that rappers can perform the task of exposing and critiquing the tension-filled ironic realities of

76

socially constructed race, class, gender, sexuality, political economy, and received knowledge. Language practices guided by this ideology are semantic extension and inversion, grammaticalization, phonological variation, and subversive spelling. In a similar vein, Smitherman (2000) discusses not only the aforementioned practices but adds narrativizing, braggadocio, playin the dozens, signifyin, and intertextuality or sampling among the communicative practices of the Hiphop Nation. Employing Afrodiasporic approaches, rappers display regional variation in U.S. Eastcoast, Westcoast, Midwest and Southern styles, and global variation of Hiphop Nation Language (HHNL), by various ethnicities that borrow, adapt and transform it throughout the world. (Alim, 2004) If one claims to be a Hiphoppa, he or she is involved in some aspect of the Hiphop elements or participates in Hiphop events on- or offline, such as purchasing recordings, learning and discussing rhymes. I turn now to an analysis of linguistic and pragmatic aspects of the practice of Hiphop as shown in online German Hiphop.

Content morpheme/codeswitching

The first language process I examine is content morpheme/codeswitching, which principally carries semantic and pragmatic information. As discussed by Myers-Scotton (2002: 41), content morphemes are usually singly occurring nouns that reflect concepts or objects not previously existing in the recipient language/culture. Content morphemes are distinguished according to whether or not they assign or receive thematic roles. So do most verbs, prepositions, and adjectives. They reflect cultural borrowing and are easily integrated into the borrowing language though they may reflect phonetic features of the source language. Cultural borrowing contrasts with core borrowing. In the latter, the word (though not the borrowed sense of it) already exists in the L1 (first language). Cultural borrowing reflects

Table 5.1 Content morphemes

aight	a.k.	Battle/battle-style	b-boy	b-girl
beats	biatch/bitch	bling bling	brotha	breaker
chill	cool(e)/kool	crew(s)	dead prez	disstracks
DJ's	eastcoast(er)	fresh(er)	flows	G's
Game	gangsta	gangsta rap	Gangsta-slang	Ghetto
hater	Hip Hop	Hiphopper	hoes	hype
ice	ill	mack	mix-CD	mixtape
Motherfucker(s)	jam	mic	nigga(z)	okay
peace/peaze	pimp	Probs/props (Ger. Sp.)	rap/raps/rapper	rap driveby
Rap shaolin	remixes	rhyme(s)	rhyme biter	Rhyme-Cypher
shoutz	skillz	sprayer	supa	tight
wanksters	weed	westcoast	word	Word Up
yo				

conscious incorporation of lexical/cultural items, which may fill lexical cultural gaps in the recipient language. In this data, there are sixty-one content morphemes.

As reported in current research, there is widespread use of Hiphop routines in German youth computer-mediated communication, such as greetings and props (Androutsopolous, 2004). In AAL/Hiphop, openings, closings, and greetings are accomplished with ritual language, such as the openings "yo" and "What(s) up?" and the closings "Peace," "I'm out," "one." Props are a form of showing respect and often include ritual recitation of names of a Hiphoppa's crew. As explained by Morgan (2001: 194), giving props involves "the recognition of influences."

Example 1: Excerpt from message board

Yo, Leudda!!!
Was geht ab?
Is echt hammerfett, dass es im Internet noch so was wie ‚n
„Zufluchtspunkt" für
HipHopper gibt.
(www.rap.de) [1999]

Gloss

Yo, people!!!
What('s) up?
It's totally awesome that there's like an asylum for Hiphoppas here in the Internet.

Example 2: Excerpt from guestbook

Yo . . . was geht'n
richtig fette Seite ich bin mittlerweile fast jeden Tag hier . . . das rockt
richtig . . .
Peazen bis dennsen und hauste
(www.rheimland.de) [2005]

Gloss

Yo . . . what's up y'all
really fat site, I've been here basically every day lately . . . it really rocks
Peace till the last and best

Example 3: Excerpt from lyrics

Yo, was geht ab, hier ist Cengiz Koc

Gloss

Yo, what('s) up this is Cengiz Koc
(TFGNK website,
http://www.20six.de/weblogCategory/117es50ayrlnu?d=29.1.2005)

Example 4: Excerpt from message board

Probs an ASCO, TKZ, Katrin, Simon, BROTHA AL, und alle
anderen Posta!
(www.rap.de) [1999]

Gloss

Props to [the above named] and all the other postas!

Example 5: Excerpt from message board

Tach
Hey nix lo shier . . . alle noch in da heia?
Shoutz an tkz oziby danphreakya asco dorian (thanx for java)
Katrin u.a.a.b.d.i.s.k. (und alle anderen boarder die ich so kenn)
Peace
(www.rap.de) [1999]

Gloss

Hey
So nothing's going on here . . . is everyone still in bed?
Shoutz to tkz oziby danphreakya asco dorian (. . .)
Katrin u.a.a.b.d.i.s.k. (and all the other boarders that I know)

Examples 1, 2, and 3 demonstrate use of Hiphop openings and closings. Both "yo" and "peaze" reflect cultural borrowings. Similarly, Examples 4 and 5 show cultural borrowings in the posters' production of the lexical items "probs" and "shoutz," which are items that reflect Hiphop's crew system. In the crew system, Hiphoppas share resources and have allegiance to each other as extended family members in whatever aspects of Hiphop they practice. (See Morgan, 2001, for detailed discussion.) Thus, the posters' performance of props shows some level of competency in and adoption of AAL/Hiphop language/literacy, even though he or she may be a consumer and not a producer. Both roles contribute to Hiphop lifestyles and musical culture.

Other content morphemes in this data reflect Hiphop's essential elements, the Hiphoppas themselves, music, basic constituents, or activities: sprayer (painter), breaker, battle, DJ's, crews, rap(per), beats, gangsta rap, gangsta-slang, Hiphoppa, b-boys, b-girls, and Rap-Fan. The aforementioned examples and those below all reflect cultural borrowing.

Example 6: Excerpt from guestbook

Hi **b-boys** und **b-girls**,
am 17.1.05 um 20.00 uhr findet ein großes treffen mit b-boy und b-girl
aus ganz deutschland stadt.
also chatet mit.
(www.breakdancecrew.de; c.f. www.rheimland.de) [2005]

Gloss

Hi b-boys and b-girls,
on January 17 at 8: 00p.m. there will be a big meeting with b-boy and
b-girl all over Germany.
So chat with us.

Example 7: Excerpt from guestbook

Alles klar auf Mukke Kontinent? Don, Ihr habt ja mittlerwile schon fast
100.000 **Crews** und **DJ** am Start, mann Jungs—also wenn Ihr demnächst
mit Eurem SL 600 zu Euer Party im Ritz fahrt, um mit hunderten con
freshen Hip-Hop Ladys, n paar Dom Perignon zu killen, dann ruft uns an!
's sagen "peace" die Torments aus dem Ländle!
(www.rheimland.de) [2005]

Gloss

Everything cool on the music continent? Don, Y'all have gotten almost
100,000 Crews and DJ at the start, man guys—so, when you next want
to drive with your SL 600 to your party, and chill with hundreds of fresh
Hip-Hop Ladys and down a couple bottles of Dom Perignon, then call us!
as the Torments from the country say, "peace!"

Example 8: Excerpt from guestbook

Deshalb was zu Deinem chat-Angebot . . . ich bin mir nicht sicher, ob isch
Disch und Deine Brüdah so ganz ohne den notwendigen derben
Gangsta-Slang aufsuchen soll . . . ich befürchte fast da würde ich ganz
bös' gedisst werden, und auf Englisch würde mich das sicher noch ne Spur
mehr verletzen (*grinz)
(www.rap.de) [1999]

Gloss

And so about your chat offer . . . I'm not sure if I want to call you and your Brothas without the necessary Gangsta-Slang . . . I'm afraid that I'd be dissed pretty bad, and in English I'm sure I would kill the Vibe even more (*grinz)

Examples 6, 7, and 8 demonstrate that Germans are active producers and participants of Hiphop. The guestbook genre is such that communicants share information and advertise as well as simply chat about Hiphop. The writer/poster in Example 6 solicits the participation of b-boys and b-girls for an event. As discussed in Smitherman (2000: 58–9) b-boys are males who "break out into a dance movement in response to the DJ's scratching of a record." This type of dance is rooted in African and Caribbean dancing and includes intricate, skilled movements of the body, including headspins to the break beat. B-girls do the same and are no less skilled. Similarly, Example 7 references "crews" and "DJ's" which are core aspects of Hiphop. The DJ spins records and is often a beat (rhythm) producer. In Example 8, a poster signals distress at his inability to use Hiphop language and therefore his marginal status. In short, though Hiphop is appropriated and recontextualized throughout the globe, these examples reflect certain core social practices that define Hiphop.

From an historical perspective, terms such as "chill" and "fresh" reflect innovations of cool by the contemporary American Hiphop generation. They may also be classified as core borrowings. Though these terms have crossed over into the mainstream and are seen as superficial style, cool represents a way of being in the world for generations of AAL speakers that is deeply connected to surviving in a complex society. As explained by Smitherman (1998: 206), "a disempowered group daily forced to face the possibility of its destruction can ill-afford to be hot." As explained by Morgan (2002: 43–4), "Coolness . . . is one of the symbolic goods that has exchange value and it can be used to accrue linguistic and pragmatic capital. One can 'lose their cool' or positive social face in interactions where participants may be culturally challenged (e.g. not know current lexical terms or meanings . . .)." "Flow" is related to "cool" as it indexes a rapper's style and ability to deliver in a rhythmically unique way lyrics that are relevant and real to the audience. Thus, "flow" is an aspect of the AAL/Hiphop ideological matrix in terms of the value placed on sound power, nommo, or the power of the word. The items "word" and "Word up" reflect this value in AAL/Hiphop and are used as a "response of affirmation." "Word Up" is also the name of a famous U.S.-based Hiphop magazine. (Smitherman, 2000: 301)

Example 9: Excerpt from lyrics

. . . du wärst gerne wie ich,
true und normal

81

kool und loyal
fresher als jeder
. . .
Ich bein wie meine nüsse alleine zu zweit
Sitze zuhaus, **chill** und mach nix, hor dann auf kiss, dirty und tight
(www.HiphopLyrics.de)

Gloss

you'd love to be like me
true and normal
kool and loyal
fresher than everyone
. . .
I sit at home, chill and do nothing, then stop and kiss, dirty and tight

Example 10: Excerpt from forum

Hab' gehört leider reichen meine **flows** nich aus!?
Doch uns're teenie groupies kennen sich mit **flows** nich aus!
(www.MZEE.com)

Gloss

I heard unfortunately my flows aren't good enough!?
Our teenie groupies don't know about flows!

Example 11: Excerpt from webpage

Word Up der Frankfurter Hip-Hop Contest wurde erstmals am 1997
ausgeschrieben. Die Gruppen müssen ihre Demotapes oder Demo-CDs
nebst eines musikalischen Lebenslaufs bis zu einem zuvor gesetzten
Stichtag an den Frankfurter Jugendring schicken. (http://www.
frankfurterjugendring.de/bilderseite-hiphop-contest.htm)

Gloss

Word Up Frankfurt Hip-Hop Contest was started for the first time in
1997. Groups must send in their Demotapes or Demo-CDs together
with a musical CV by a previously set deadline to Frankfurt youth ring.

Example 9 is taken from the lyrics of "Don't Hate" by Kool Savas, who has been
compared to Eminem. According to a Wikipedia entry for German Hiphop,
"[Kool Savas] sports aggressive and intricate, but often homophobic and misogynist

battle rhymes." He is known for collaborating with African American rappers such as Kurupt, and Royce da 5′9″. It is no surprise then that his rap would reflect the boastful aggressive style and outlaw persona that is the hallmark of many successful AAL/Hiphoppas. Example 10 is taken from MZEE.com, which boasts of being the largest German-speaking Hiphop medium of all. The short excerpt here came from a section called the "Rhyme-Cypher." In it, developing or practicing rappers try out their rhyming skills while other participants comment and evaluate. The rapper/writer in this example raps about his "flow" being uncomprehended by groupie girls. What is noteworthy here is that flow is a criterion for judging performance in the German context as in the original AAL/Hiphop context. Example 11 demonstrates that "Word Up" is a response of affirmation in the German context as well. "Word Up" as the name for the German Hiphop contest validates the contest and its winners as authentic.

Solidarity with the streets or those who have been historically downtrodden is integral to Hiphop consciousness. Despite the fact that many Hiphop participants and consumers did not grow up in ghettoes, most have experienced violence or at least lack of self-confidence on some level. "Reality rap," alternatively titled "gangsta rap," reflects street consciousness. Keyes (2002: 125), following sociologist Eugene Perkins, identified key personalities associated with street culture: "street man, hustler, pimp (or mack), working-class man, and militant," noting that "gangsta" or "thug" is also recognized by rap artists of both genders who sometimes portray these characters. Furthermore, Keyes (2002: 125) argues that "the conceptual base of rap music is rooted in a street style." I would add to Keyes' conceptual base the concept or practice of Blackness, or at least awareness of race and ethnicity, as these play a significant role in one's street experiences. During the writing of this chapter, rapper 50 Cent, noted for his gritty street and pimped-out rhymes, was number one on the MTV German Hitlist with his single "Candy Shop," outplacing Germany's mega rap band Fettes Brot, at number 5, with their single "Emanuele." (http://www.mtvhome.de/hitlistgermany/index.php) Lexical items such as bitch/biatch, G's, gangsta, hater, hoes, pimp, mack, motherfuckers, nigga, and supa are common in such performances. These terms would be considered cultural borrowings.

Example 12: Excerpt from website

Fick, was ihr über mein Image denkt
Ich bin nicht Ja Rule **Motherfucker's**
Und Ihr seid ganz bestimmt nicht 50 Cent
Ihr **Wanksters** givt mir mein Respect wieder her

Gloss

Fuck, what y'all think of my image
I'm not Ja Rule motherfuckers

And you are so not 50 Cent
You wanksters give me my respect over here

These lyrics were posted on the website of "The Fucking German Nazi Kids" (TFGNK). They are from the song "Die Abrechnung" by Eko Fresh.[6] "Motherfucker" in the AAL/Hiphop context refers to "a person, place, an event . . . either negatively or positively depending on the context" (Smitherman, 2000: 204) and "wanksters" was made popular by African American rapper 50 Cent. It refers to a fake gangsta, someone who will crack under pressure and who cannot command street credibility. Bakari Kitwana's inclusion of "Wangsta" in the title of his latest book *Why White Kids Love Hip Hop: Wangstas, Wiggers, Wannabes, and the New Reality of Race in America* (2005)—signals its widespread use in the American context. In the German context, the term may not be as widespread. There has been no shortage of conversations concerning the translatability and the global transmission of Black musics to places that are scarcely populated by Blacks or that have totally different social systems. Yet "global" rappers and rap fans use AAL/Hiphop terms such as these that are highly identifiable with original Hiphop. According to Eko Fresh's biography, he is comparable to 50 Cent and has been called the King of Germany, though he is seen as inauthentic by some German Hiphoppas. His biography states:

Oberstes Stockwerk eines Hochhauses in Mönchengladbach, der Vater hat sich früh aus dem Staub gemacht, immerhin aber das Gymnasium durfte es sein, zumindest bis die Rap-Karriere rief. Die typische deutsche Rap-Sozialisation eben, die nur bei den noch härteren Jungs aus Berlin manchmal auf Unverständnis stößt. Zu wenig Ghetto. Eko selfbst ist das ungefähr so egal wie die Tatsache, dass sich Uneingeweihte über die herrlich provokante Reimlosigkeit mancher seiner Featureparts aufregen: "Ich schäme mich weder für die Tatsache, dasshich auf dem Gymnasium war, noch dafür, dass ich aus Mönchengladbach komme."
    (http://www.chart-radio.de/viewartistbio.php3?interpret=eko+fresh)

At the top floor of a high rise in Mönchengladbach, his father bolted early, but all the same he went to high school, at least until the rap-career took off. The typical German rap socialization at any rate, which only doesn't come across to the harder core guys in Berlin. Not enough ghetto. Eko himself cares about that as much as he cares about the fact that the non-enlightened get upset about the delicious non-rhymingness of his features: "I'm not ashamed of the fact that I went to high school or that I'm from Mönchengladbach."

One glaring stereotype in Eko's biography is the premise that being educated is anti-Hiphop. Thus, he has to justify that he is a real Hiphoppa despite the fact that he finished high school. One need only know Hiphop's elements to understand that knowledge is respected and highly admired among the groups (Black Caribbeans, Latinos, and Black Americans) from which Hiphop originally developed. Not respected in the hoods are people who have formal education but no wisdom, those who have lost touch with the struggles of everyday people. Eko's statement reflects that he is aware of the dominant stereotypical understanding of Hiphop. Berns and Schlobinski (2003) examine German rappers' adoption of gangsta style through analysis of the rap lyrics of the group Midnite Sonz. They report (2003: 204) that the group "import[ed] patterns of Afro-American vernacular culture without properly adapting them." This resulted in their inability to gain credibility among Germans, as evidenced by their failure to attract a national audience, their invisibility on the underground scene, and their inability to secure a deal with a record company. Berns and Schlobinski write (2003: 205):

> In our view, this can be attributed to the attitude they chose to adopt. Specifically, topics such as violence, drug-dealing and illegal business are usually regarded as reflections of ghetto-like living conditions, where the language is harsh because the living is harsh. However, none of these ghetto problems exist in Germany.

From the sources that I was able to consult, this is not the case for Eko Fresh and Kool Savas, both whom have been identified with the American gangsta rap genre. Kool Savas even uses "nigga" in his raps, a controversial term stemming from the history of slavery, racism, and White supremacy; yet, this term has been semantically manipulated, reappropriated, and policed by Blacks. As discussed by Smitherman (2000) "nigga" has a variety of meanings, both positive and negative, and can refer to a Black male or female. Blacks often use the term to refer to Whites, as does Denzel Washington's notorious dirty cop character in the film *Training Day*. (He repeatedly calls his White partner "my nigga.") On the other hand, many Black people do not accept uses of the term by Whites and those outside of Black culture (and even unfamiliar Black folks). Below is an occurrence of the term in Kool Savas' song "Ihr Müsst Noch Üben" (Y'all Still Gotta Practice):

> Yo, Yo Nutte blas zuende, meine Zeit is knapp gemessen
> Deine Mutter wartet draussen und will Penis in die Fresse
> **Nigga**, laß die Faxen, deine Crew sind alles Punker

> Yo, Yo finish the blowjob, my time's running out
> Your mother's waiting outside and wants penis in her mouth
> Nigga, stop fooling around, your crew is all punks

Androutsopolous (2004) argues that terms such as "nigga" should be regarded as instances of language crossing as defined by Rampton (1995) whereby a speaker consciously uses language that is stereotypically identified with another group, in this case African Americans. He further states that "nigga" "has a local meaning by virtue of its uncommonness and the indexing of 'original' hip-hop culture . . . emphatically [presenting] the writer (and his addressees) as a community of engaged hip-hop fans." I think this is important to point out in relation to the Hiphop paradigm. The rapper, Savas, prides himself on being a battle rapper which calls for the use of strong words that will move the crowd. Though he might get a pass from the German rap crowd, intimate African American rappers, and perhaps American rap fans if/when he is collaborating with Kurupt and Royce da 5'9", currently his usage would be problematic with unfamiliar Blacks or a Black non-rap audience. In other words, because of his audience, the genre, and his personal style, his use of "nigga" as shown above is not remarkable and presents an odd case of language crossing. Further, as a rapper of migrant descent, Savas (and other migrant rappers) legitimizes his appropriation of "nigga" by drawing an analogy between the social conditions of migrants in Germany and those of Afro-Americans in the U.S. (Androutsopolous, personal communication) This is not to say that the historical experiences are the same or that Blacks in America and migrants to Germany hold the same values, but that some German Hiphoppas identify with aspects of that struggle. On the other hand, we should never underestimate the fact that American Hiphop is a money maker and it is no surprise that people from around the globe wanna get paid.

At the time of writing, Kool Savas was number forty-eight (with "Monstershit") on MTV's Hitlist Germany and had been on the charts for fifty-five weeks. This indicates that a large number of German Hiphoppas are feelin his Germanized AAL/Hiphop flow.

To summarize my discussion of content morphemes, all of those presented here are cultural borrowings and reflect German Hiphoppas' engagement with various core AAL/Hiphop language, literacy, and social practices, even as they use German language and context. I turn now to a discussion of code mixing.

System morpheme/code mixing

System morphemes are a set of inflections and function words that come from the morpho-syntax, according to the Matrix Language Frame (MLF) model. The ML is the language that frames the utterance, often the L1, but not necessarily (Myers-Scotton, 2002). Bokamba (1988: 245) defines code mixing as: "the embedding or mixing of various linguistic units, i.e., affixes, words, phrases, and clauses from two distinct grammatical systems or subsystems within the same sentence and the same speech situation."

Under the MLF model, it should be noted that the projection of complementizer (CP) (rather than the sentence) offers more precise observation of the ML framing the syntactic structure of an utterance (can be any clause in which the complementizer is null or fully realized). (Myers-Scotton, 2002) In this particular data, the ML is usually German. The German speakers/writers have enough proficiency in AAL to realize AAL lexis in mixed constituents framed by German, or to produce well-formed AAL chunks, or both.

Table 5.2 Code mixing/integration

aufpimpen	Brüdah
Bomben	purem beat
Abchecken	deine mama tanzt nach meiner crack pfeife
Chillt fette	Gangstamucke
Chillige Grüß	Gangsta texte
Mich disst/disste mich/gedissed/zu	Hammerhartes Ghetto-image
dissen/gedisst	Hip-hop gemeinde
Freshen Hip-Hop Ladys	Hip Hop Gott
Zu chillen	ist der shit (is da shit)
droppt	richtige niggaz
gedopest	Texte drop
flowt	Milchschnitten-Rapper posier
gehate/gehatet/gehated	Shoutz an
rapst/rapt/gerappt	Singsang-Rap-Kastastrophenalarm
spittest	Straight aus dem Ruhrpott (straight outta
der wackste	Ruhrpott)
	Yo mein rap is phat wie deine mama

There are 41 examples of code mixing in this data. The items in the left-hand column can be analyzed as integrated borrowing of AAL/Hiphop lexical morphemes with German system morphemes.

Example 13: Excerpt from a message board and posted lyrics

The example below contains German word forms of AAL/Hiphop "diss." In AAL/Hiphop, "diss" is a verb, meaning to disrespect someone (Smitherman, 2000) or to "reject, ignore, and embarrass". (Morgan, 2001: 200) Further, it is a rap trope. (Morgan, 2002: 53) The examples below retain these original senses.

a) Ich befürchte fast da würde ich ganz bös' **gedisst** warden
   (I'm afraid that I'd be dissed pretty bad)
   (www.rap.de message board) [1999]

b) Ihr habt mich all zuertst **gedissed**!
   (Y'all dissed me first)
   (Eko Fresh on TFGNK website)

c) Mein Wortschatz von 10 Wörten für Scheiße reicht noch dicke um
   dich **zu dissen**
   (My vocabulary of 10 words for shit is still plenty to diss you)
   (STF feat. Kool Savas on www.HipHopLyrics.de)

d) Bushido **disste mich**
   (Bushido dissed me)
   (Eko Fresh on TFGNK website)

Examples 13a and b, "gedisst" and "gedissed," reflect a case of spelling variation, where first form is orthographically integrated. In 13a, the writer is worried that he/she will be dissed in a proposed future chat with Hiphop insiders, thus conveying his/her lack of insider knowledge and skills. 13b is from "Die Abrechnung" (Settling the Score) by Eko Fresh. In this line of the song he justifies the lyrical whipping he is unleashing on rappers with whom he has beef (conflict). 13c, "zu dissen," is an infinitive form of the verb, where "zu" is a preposition meaning "to" and the "-en" suffix indicates the infinitive form. This example is from the lyrics of Kool Savas' "Ihr Müst Noch Üben," (Y'all Still Gotta Practice), a song which emphasizes Savas' lyrical skills and superior masculinity. In 13d the "-te" affixed to AAL/Hiphop "diss" indicates the preterite (past tense). This line is also from the aforementioned Eko Fresh tune. Additional AAL/Hiphop loanwords that retain their original usage and exhibit German integration are "hate," "rap," and "chill".

Example 14: Excerpts from lyrics

a) Ich Hab Die Krone Wieder, Ihr Habt Genug **Gehated**-oder-Ich
   Sette Trends, honey
   (I got the crown/mic again, y'all have hated enough-or-I set trends, honey)
   (www.MZEE.com forum)
b) danach kommt von dir moistens nur **gehate**
   EY du scheißt auf jeden Jack
   (and after that from you it's mostly hate
   Hey you're shitting on every Jack)
   (Eko Fresh on TFGNK website)
c) Ihr habt genug **gehatet**
   (Y'all have hated enough)
   (Eko Fresh on TFGNK website)

In AAL/Hiphop "hate" or "hate on [somebody]" is a verb expressing envy through words. (Smitherman, 2000: 159) This verb is used accordingly in the German. The above examples of mixing show German morphological integration of "hate" using system morphemes "ge-" for past participle as in 14a. Example 14b, "gehate," is an abstract noun; there is a regular formation pattern in German, which generates abstract nouns from verb stems by the combination of the prefix "Ge-" + stem + suffix "-e" (sometimes zero suffix). The pattern's meaning is, roughly, "continuous V / repeated V". This compares to the nominalized use of "hating". In 14c perfective participle, "ge-" for past tense.

The examples in the right-hand column of Table 5.2 exhibit various mixing of German adjectives, prepositions, pronouns, and nouns with AAL/Hiphop lexical items.

Example 15: Excerpt from message board

Deshalb was zu Deinem chat-Angebot . . . ich bin mir nicht sicher, ob isch Disch und Deine **Brüdah** so ganz ohne den notwendigen derben Gangsta-Slang aufsuchen soll . . . ich befürchte fast, da würde ich ganz bös' gedisst werden, und auf Englisch würde mich das sicher noch ne Spur mehr verletzen (*grinz)
(www.rap.de) [1999]

Gloss

And so about your chat offer . . . I'm not sure if I want to call you and your Brothas without the necessary Gangsta-Slang . . . I'm afraid that I'd be dissed pretty bad, and in English I'm sure I would kill the Vibe even more (*grinz)

"Brüdah" is a hybrid which mixes AAL/Hiphop "brotha" with German "bruder" captured in the AAL/Hiphop spelling (Androutsopolous, 2004). In AAL, "brotha" refers to Black men. In the online message board example, the race of the writers is not known; however, it appears that it is used by those who are or want to be identified as real or original Hiphoppas of any race/nation.

Example 16: Excerpt from message board

My favorite example of mixing is: "Yo mein Rap is phat wie deine Mama." This example contains the AAL discourse practice of the dozens or snaps, defined by Smitherman as the verbal game of insult, usually directed at the mother. The first mixed constituent is "mein rap." Another is "deine mama." It appears that "is phat" makes the ML English and not German; however, "is" represents orthographically the colloquial pronunciation of "ist" undergoing consonant cluster simplification. This example, employing as it does the dozens, makes clear an important point not just about the integration of AAL/Hiphop in German but also about the discourse practices of Hiphop. Although I am not here focusing on the discourse/communicative style of German Hiphoppas, I have found examples of oppositional language, the dozens, signifying, dissin, and boasting/braggadocio in German Hiphop discourse; hallmarks of Hiphop discourse.

Example 17: Excerpts from lyrics

a) Ich hör **Gangsta Texte**, Gangsta Rap
   (I listen to gangsta lyrics, gangsta rap)

b) durch die Stadt, **Gangstamucke** bei Nacht
(Through the city, gangsta gigs in the night)
(www.ksavas.de/ksavas/index.htm)

c) Leider zu viele Rapper, die keine sind, denn sie singen bloß—
Diskussion sinnlos
Singsang-Rap-Katastrophenalarm bei Eurem Auftritt
(Unfortunately too many rappers, who aren't, because they sing—
Useless discussion.
Rap red alert upon your entrance)
(www.HiphopLyrics.de)

"Gangsta Texte" (17a) comprises the AAL/Hiphop item "gangsta"—reference to outlaw style of rap music and aesthetic—and the German nominative plural "texte." The literal translation would be "gangsta lyrics," a German coinage or at least an uncommon usage in AAL. Considering that this line is from a song, the rapper is taking poetic license. I would argue that "texte" is the preference of Kool Savas. Similarly, 17b, "Gangstamucke," consists of AAL/Hiphop "Gangsta" and the German slang term for music, "mucke." Another creative example of mixture from lyrics in this data is 17c, "Singsang-rap-Kastastrophenalarm," from 808 Mafia's "Am Tag danach zu Spät," which is a noun compound.

Another language practice that illustrates German creativity within a paradigm of both German language production and original Hiphop ideology is embedded language.

Embedded language/codeswitching

Embedded language (EL) relies on the donor language for structure and contains two or more morphemes, showing hierarchical relationship. They must be well formed in the EL, in which case they are called EL islands (Myers-Scotton, 2002: 54). Sally Boyd's (1997: 261) definition is also helpful:

> the phonology, morphology and syntax of the EL material follows EL grammar, not ML grammar . . . Also, . . . no claims are made as to recurrence of switching in the wider community; and . . . code-switching often involves longer stretches of speech in EL, but in a limiting case may also be applied to single words.

Example 18: Excerpt from lyrics

most wanted rapper bei wom **drop hits** wie bomben und fliege davon
(most wanted rapper at WOM drop hits like bombs and fly out from them)
(http://www.ksavas.de/ksavas/index.htm)

Table 5.3 Embedded language

Best Flows	peace out
Big shout out	Peace shout
Da Masta is back	Pimp My Ride/Pimp My Stereo
drop hits	Pop-Rap-Clowns
German Dream Baby	Pseudo Hip-Hop Fan
Peace to all the hardcore headz	"Stick Up Kid"
how you livin on your block?	The dopest mc on da mic!
I'm out!	wack Rhymes
keep it real/keep it rollin!	weak nigga
Keep ya headz up	Yeah b-Style
krasse Gettho	yeah, yo
Krasse style	Yo, to all tha mc's
maximum respect	PEACE to da NorthEast!
most wanted rapper	PeAcE N.I.G.G.A.

Example 19: From guestbook

Würdet ihr nicht auch liebend gerne mal euer Auto so richtig *aufpimpen*?
Doch euch fehlt die Kohle?
Habt ihr schon etliche Bewerbungen zu **Pimp My Ride** geschickt?
Und es kam nie eine Antwort zurück?
Oder laufen in euren alten Tapedecks immer doch diese
durchgeleierten Sekte Tapes?
Dann haben BEATWARS & Da KID genau das richtige für euch!
PIMP MY STEREO!!
(www.rap.de) [1999]

Gloss

Wouldn't y'all love to get your ride pimped?
But you don't have the cash?
Have you tried to beg Pimp My Ride yet?
And didn't get an answer?
Are there really still these shitty tapes running in your tape decks?
Then BEATWARS & DA KID have just the right thing for you!
PIMP MY STEREO!!

Example 20: Excerpt from guestbook

Von c-town!!**how you livin on your block**? Ist deine auch hot?
(Of c-town!!how you livin on your block? Is yours hot too?)
(www.rap.de) [1999]

Example 18 represents a semantically or pragmatically motivated EL island. Again, the rapper, Kool Savas, is boasting. In this song, "Don't Hate," he is performing with African American rappers, which might be an added impetus for him to insert language associated with original Hiphop culture, further legitimizing his status as authentic. Example 19 shows the influence of German MTV, which has segments taken over directly from American television as well as German productions (Covell Waegner, 2004). *Pimp My Ride* is a popular MTV show. In AAL/Hiphop when someone or something is pimped out, it means well dressed, excellent. The web writer in the above example solicits customers for a stereo business with a name influenced by *Pimp My Ride* which will be appealing to the Hiphop audience/ market. Example 20 ("how you livin on your block?") demonstrates a case where AAL/Hiphop is the Matrix Language according to Myers-Scotton's MLF theory, as the morpho-syntax follows AAL and not German. The zero copula and the utterance's semantic frame suggest AAL/Hiphop. The usage signals the writer/ poster's wish to engage other participants in conversation about what is happening in their locales. Opening and closing routines are notable in the embedded language examples. Openings: yeah, yo; yo to all tha mc's, big shout out; Peace to all the hardcore headz. Closings: I'm out; maximum respect; peace out; peace shout; peace N.I.G.G.A. Also represented in embedded language are slogans, such as the Hiphop mantra "Keep it real."

Calquing

The final language process that I will discuss is calquing, whereby semantic adaptation of loanwords occurs and they are translated without phonetic (orthographic) adjustment into the lexicon of the recipient language. (T'sou, 1975: 448) Table 5.4 displays fourteen calqued items.

Table 5.4 Calques

German Expression	AAL/HH	Mode
Bin draussen!/bin raus/draussen	I'm out/out	guestbook poster
das ist fett	dass phat	forum poster
dien Hund	yo(ur) dawg	Eko lyrics
die schärfsten Ischen	da hottes chicks	Savas lyrics
dicksten	phattes	Savas lyrics
fette	phat	guestbook poster
fette grüß	phat greetings	guestbook poster
fette Gratulation	phat congratulation	guestbook poster
freistil	freestyle	guestbook poster
harte kern	hardcore	808 Mafia lyrics
ich fließ	I'm flowing	Savas lyrics
lyrische härte	lyrical hardness	forum poster
mach wir unsern ding	let's do our thing	Savas lyrics
respekt	respect	Eko lyrics

"Bin draussen," "bin raus," and "draussen" are the German forms of a ritual Hiphop closing, "I'm out" or "out."

Example 21: Excerpt from guestbook

Alle anderen . . . Keep ya headz up!
Bin draussen! . . .
PEACE! ASCO!
(www.rap.de) [1999]

Gloss

To everyone else . . . Keep ya headz up!
I'm out! . . .
PEACE! ASCO!

In AAL/Hiphop respect is an integral part of the culture. Respect involves recognizing and acknowledging someone's worth, authenticity, skill, or style. The greeting "respect" is a part of the Hiphop system, as is giving props. In that German "respekt" has taken on AAL/Hiphop semantics and pragmatics we might say that "respekt" is rather a case of "loan meaning." In other words, the meaning and pragmatics of respect has been widened to align to the use of AAL/Hiphop.

Example 22: Excerpt from lyrics

Fick, was ihr über mein Image denkt,
Ich bin nicht Ja Rule Motherfucker's
Und Ihr seid ganz bestimmt nicht 50 Cent
Ihr Wanksters gibt mir mein **Respekt** wieder her
(http://www.20six.de/weblogCategory/117es50ayrlnu?d=29.1.2005)

Gloss

Fuck, what y'all think of my image
I'm not Ja Rule motherfuckers,
And you are so not 50 cent
You wanksters, give me my respect on over here

Similarly, 'your *dog*' is a friend or associate. (Smitherman, 2000: 111)

Example 23: Excerpt from lyrics

Nicon ist **dein Hund**, du sagst es und er scheißt in dein Glas
(Nicon is your dog, you say it and he shits in your glass)
(Eko Fresh's lyrics on TFGNK website)

Other examples of calques include "fette" or "dicksten" to indicate high evaluation, as AAL/Hiphop "phat." "Freistil" is a mode of Hiphop discourse, whereby one's raps are unrehearsed and spontaneous, "freestyle." It should not be surprising that the rapper Kool Savas employs this term, or practices the craft.

Rapper/producer Wyclef Jean shouted from his mic at a rap concert, "Where my Asian niggas? Where my white niggas? Where my Latino niggas? Where my Black niggas?" Each of Wyclef's calls was met by increasingly deafening affirmative cheers. It was awkward because though all of these groups were in the same hall, listening to the same music, they were segregated into mostly racially based crews and peers—the White Americans with same, a few Asians appeared to be mixed in with Latinos, and a few Latinos with the Blacks, but mostly I noticed the distinct segregation of each group in the crowd. Specifically, I recall the nervous snickers and the eyes of the youth searching to see how other groups responded to their identification of themselves as "niggas." Experiencing the music and each other together is a lot different than experiencing it through videos, CDs, and other global technologies. An African American female rap activist related to me that she had to check (correct) a little Japanese Hiphoppa who greeted her in Japan with "What's up my nigga?" She had to explain to him that she didn't play that.

In treating the problem of crossover and acquisition of Afrodiasporic practices to wider audiences in the American context, several studies of language, identity, and Hiphop have discussed the acquisition of AAL by speakers of other language varieties/languages (Bucholz, 1997; Cutler, 1997; Ibrahim, 2003). The cultural prestige of AAL/Hiphop is identified as one impetus for acquisition or use of AAL/Hiphop. In the international context, some scholars acknowledge the major influence of resistance strategies of Afrodiasporic aesthetics in "global Hiphop." For example, Ayhan Kaya (2002) discusses a Turkish rap group's semantic inversion of the term "Kan-Ak," usually spelled "Kanak/Kanake," as a parallel to AAL/Hiphop redefinition of "nigga." "Kanak," now a widely used label for second-generation migrants (mostly, but not only, Turks) who resist the discriminative and assimilationist views of dominant German society, originally a term of abuse towards foreigners, has been reappropriated and upgraded by migrants themselves—hence the parallel to "nigga."[7] Such youth employ AAL as a means of imagining themselves as a part of a transnational/global Hiphop nation. Yasemin Yildiz discusses this phenomenon as it is exemplified in *Kanak Sprak: 24Mißtöne vom Rande der Gesellschaft*, by the Turkish German writer, Feridun Zaimoglu, containing monologues of twenty-four Turkish German youth. Yildiz (2004: 328) writes:

> The English words, "breaker" "posse" and "peace," stem from the vocabulary of African American rap culture and in the speech of this [German breakdancer] provide an identity, a community, and a vision, respectively. Beyond the referential meaning of the words, they offer a mode of orientation and of making sense of the world, of one's own

position within it as well as a "code" of conduct. This orientation and sense-making activity draws on a social analysis implicit in the terms themselves. Because of these implicit meanings, German words could not take their place.

African American aesthetics are also drawn upon: "[by] mixing traditional Turkish musical instruments like the zurna, baglama and ud with the Afro-American drum-computer rhythm, [Turkish rap groups] transculturate rap music." (Kaya, 2002: 52) Parallel aesthetic formations have also been discussed by Tony Mitchell (2001: 202). For example, in his discussion of Italian rap, Mitchell identifies traditions of ritual insult among washerwomen as a source for the dozens and "flyting" as a parallel to signifying in Italian rap. He draws attention to various Italian folk music traditions, Mediterranean, African, African American, Jamaican and Anglo-American social and musical practices that comprise Italian rap music. According to Mitchell, "appropriation of Jamaican and black American vocal styles saw words like *rappare*, *scratchare*, and *ragga* enter the Italian language, and *rispetto* (respect) and *nella casa* (in the house) take on new specific meanings." An issue for some scholars of international rap and no doubt some rap and Hiphop participants is: given American rap's globalization, isn't it essentialist to call it Black?

From the examples of written discourse that I have analyzed in online contexts some conclusions are obvious. First, the various types of language incorporation make it clear that German Hiphoppas adopt elements and concepts of AAL/Hiphop through their consumption and production of Hiphop culture. As Sherif Hetata (1998: 279) argues, "The United States produces two-thirds of all the media images in the world. The media culture of the United States is an integral part of global culture, global power, and the global economy." Many are of the opinion that commodification reduces the resistance art aspect of Hiphop to a style and image, appropriating it as a mere profitable commodity. Media plays a major role, and, as argued by T'sou (1975: 450), the language recipient's access to mass media provides the contact necessary for linguistic and cultural assimilation, even when such recipients may be far removed geographically from the host society or culture. Because commercial distribution of rap and Hiphop culture does not flow back into the U.S. as easily as it circulates out of the U.S., the circumstances of international contact prevent mutual influence, though there is some. However, each culture brings its own history and social practices to the sociocultural formations of Hiphop. Second, though this data shows language crossing, the meaning of this crossing is not always clear without more intimate knowledge of who is writing or rappin what, to whom, and under what conditions. Certain Hiphop practitioners are accepted as authentic users of AAL/Hiphop, while others are not. As I have tried to show in this chapter, Hiphop carries with it a paradigm, an aesthetic, and ideologies brought about through culture-specific sociopolitical and economic realities. Our language and culture have been diffused in several ways via various media and technologies. People from around the globe are free to take up these expressions and transform them to fit their own realities; as Murray

Forman argues, "the hood comes first." At the same time, the hood that came first was a Bronx hood. A major goal of this chapter has been to document the contribution that African American Hiphop has contributed to youth identity around the world. This examination of the global reach of Black youth cultural resiliency and creativity should inspire us to remillion[8] our efforts to nurture and elevate them to new heights.

6

HIPHOP AND VIDEO GAMES

As commercial rap music and Hiphop elements are incorporated into all manner of global media and businesses, the union of Hiphop and video games should come as no surprise. With today's highly advanced technologies, graphics, and sounds, video games have the ability to provide images and experiences that s(t)imulate, delight, and excite players. It is estimated that about 60 percent of Americans play video games. (Glaubke *et al.*, 2001) The games industry takes in about 18 billion a year. (Jones, 2005: C1) In Great Britain over 26 million video games were sold in 1999, and they are even more popular in Japan. (Spina, 2004) Hiphop is providing a source of meaning and identification to people the world over. Writing of the sudden interest in developing "urban and hip-hop themes" in video games, one writer comments that the 2004 Electronic Entertainment Expo (E3) was the "'thugging' of the games industry." ("Thug Life": 40) In 2003, the biggest-selling PlayStation 2 (PS2) game was Madden NFL 2004. The second-best selling game that year was Need for Speed Underground. Both are urban themed. ("Thug Life": 40) Two video games centered on Hiphop are Get On Da Mic and Get On Da Floor.[1] These are both produced by a company called Eidos. Another of their games is 25 to Life, which can be played on XBOX, PS2, and PC platforms. It is rated M (for mature audiences) by the Entertainment Software Ratings Board (ESRB) because it contains "blood and gore," "drug references," "intense violence," "sex themes," and "strong language." Rob Dyer, president of Eidos, thinks that successful video games are the ones "that tap into something from real life. Hip-hop is an extension of the aspirational lifestyle, and there's definitely a groundswell of games right now that all tap into this culture." ("Thug Life": 40)

Just as with other industries that have appropriated Hiphop, the gaming industry is a double-edged sword. From one perspective, this industry offers unprecedented opportunities for young people of color to market certain insider knowledge. For example, the makers of Grand Theft Auto San Andreas approached 50 Cent about doing some voice work for one of their characters. 50 (Curtis Jackson) and the cofounder of Interscope Records, Jimmy Iovine, were savvy enough to turn that down and get Vivendi Universal to model an entire game, Bulletproof, on 50's life story. In this way, "The game provides 50 with a cross-promotion bonanza. All the products he designs or endorses—G-Unit clothing, Reebok sneakers, Glaceau

Vitaminwater—appear in Bulletproof." (Jones, 2005: C1) His videos and his music are pumped through this video game. From another perspective, there is controversy over issues of representation, realism, and stereotyping in the games. What are some of the components of digital Blackness as experienced through Hiphop video games? This chapter offers a brief foray into some literacy practices engaged in playing these games.

James Gee argues that good video games challenge their players to apply their conceptual knowledge. A player must take on an identity that the game presents, learn the rules of the game and apply them appropriately. Gee cites several cognitive principles that accompany learning: identity, interaction, production, risk taking, customization, agency, well-ordered problems, challenge and consolidation, "just-in-time and on demand," situated meanings, pleasantly frustrating, system thinking, "explore, think laterally, rethink goals . . . smart tools, distributed knowledge," and cross-functional teams. (Gee, 2003) Gee is interested in the model that video games provide for learning. My interest is slightly different. I am interested in what people already know, their worldly literacies and the ideological viewpoints manifested by interacting with video games that exploit Hiphop content—symbology, music, language, and landscape. For the purposes of this study, I will exploit Gee's principles of identity, interaction, production, and agency. The identity principle states that players commit to an identity, by which I mean one that is unquestionably associated with the world of the game, and for our purposes that world will have some connection to how Hiphop is understood in the world. Players must interact with the game in order to initiate the finite permutations of action and language that are given within the context and domain of the virtual world. As producers, players co-construct the game by the choices and actions that they make and take. Players have agency when playing well-constructed video games. To the extent that video-game texts project various objects and perspectives by means of color, setting, sounds, printed words, depictions, etc., I am interested in multimodality. In other words, these combined media create new ways of making meaning and perhaps a different kind of meaning.(Hull and Nelson, 2005)

To get into this virtual world, I will here focus on one game in particular, Def Jam Vendetta. This game is made for the PS2 console. Sony, the Japanese electronics company giant (that is still a White corporation[2]), manufactures PlayStation, which is the world's biggest-selling home-game console. (Blacksoftware.com) I chose this game because it includes simulated rappers, draws on Hiphop aesthetics, and has wide appeal. The analysis offered here is not meant to be exhaustive, but another example of the rock and hard place that Hiphop is in. As eloquently stated by Bakari Kitwana (2005: 48)

> What comes out of the corporate hip-hop industry is packaged and sold as hip-hop, but it is a distortion of hip-hop culture.
> With so many whites working in the hip-hop industry, naturally the final product would appeal to other white kids. Those hip-hop industry insiders, like everyone else, grew up socialized in American culture. That

culture informs their thinking . . . Most things offensive to mainstream tastes aren't going to saunter past these gatekeepers. Whether it offends Black people . . . is another matter. But if it's offensive to the mainstream you can be sure it won't break through . . . it's a cultural and financial imperative.

Def Jam Vendetta

Used to be you wanted to make yourself known, you'd prove your worth as a street fighter or a hustler. We don't fight out in tha streets no mo. We're organized now. We . . . too gangsta for the garden, so we takin it underground, inside. I'm a businessman and this is my biznass. My souljahs are legion: Method Man, Nore, Capone, Luda, Redman, DMX. You wanna shot at me, you gotta make it pass these bruthas. It's a dangerous world out here. It seems evrytime I turn around, there's another young buck wants to take me on. I lay down for no man. You wanna take what's mine, you gotta beat me; but nobody evaahh beats me. Def Jam Vendetta.[3]

The above narration is delivered in a commanding, deep-toned male voice. It works as the root narrative of the game and points to certain street and underground economies outside of the mainstream market which allow its participants to earn money, power, and respect. The visuals that accompany this narrative introduction to the world of the underground wrestling game include fast cars and SUVs, one with dark-tinted windows and a sexy lightskinned woman, with flowing curls and Anglo-oriented features, looking at the player through her swiftly up-rolling window. At first, the camera's perspective slowly reveals to the player a dark blue night in the urban terrain. Then it zooms (like a fast car) past bright lights, tall buildings, over bridges and the river into the world down under, into what looks like a warehouse that has been remodeled into the two-tier simulated Def Jam South sports arena, complete with boxing ring. The player enters the underground world of fighting through graffiti-marked corridors postered with ads containing hard-bodied males to advertise fights. Urbanly clad males[4] (some in fatigues) and (ghetto-fabulously styled) females hangin in the halls, a man and a woman embracing each other. The features of the male characters are mostly exaggerated, bulging muscles, seedy eyes, huge foreheads, and wide mouths, more cartoonish than minstrel-like. The arena is filled with cheering spectators, including beautifully well-drawn females (thin waists, flowing hair, and shapely hips) and to add to the scenery are the sponsors' logos: Def Jam and Phat Farm. This game is about fighting and all of the characters possess commanding physical presence, and aim for spiritual, psychological, and bodily domination. White fighters are represented in this scene too. They also have hard bodies, tattoos, bulging muscles, exaggerated features. They come across as industrial types by their wearing of plaid shirts, bandannas, and wife beaters. They don't walk like *Fortune* 500 men. They appear hardened by their work. Some have black marker under their eyes like football players. It is the world of bucks, in terms of cash and testosterone. According to the game's liner notes, "Def Jam Vendetta brings together the shady and dangerous worlds of hard-core hip-hop and underground fighting. Go head to head with some of the toughest and meanest brutes the street has to offer." The musical score accompanying the visuals is serious. The sounds of polyrhythmic drums, high hats, and strings intertwined with city sounds, auto horns, sirens, traffic, and city bustle invite the player into a head-nodding groove of the actual game by way of the virtual. The official soundtrack is stimulating and provided by Def Jam recording artists. Tracks such as DMX's "Party Up" (remember "Y'all gone make me lose my mind up in here, up in here"), Method Man's "Bring the Pain," Noreaga's "Nothin," and Public Enemy's "Fight the Power" stand out, among others.

In the main menu, one of the choices of mode of play is "Story." In this mode, one can play singly and "fight for money, power and respect; unlock new characters and venues." The second menu choice is "Battle," symbolized by a fist, where up to four players can play. Here you can "Bring your crew and throw down." An ugly skull presents the next choice—"Survival." When entering it, a voice asks, "You think you got what it takes to survive?" The accompanying text reads, "Just you against the world." How appropriate. In the fourth menu choice, "Tutorial," new players can get explanations of the health of their fighters, how to work the controls, how to execute different types of attack, how to grapple, throw an opponent down, move on the mat, and how to gain momentum. This game is definitely geared toward males. The fifth menu choice—"Galleries,"—allows the successful player to "Check out shots of all the fly honeys . . . picked up." The options allow the player to adjust sound effects, speech, volume of music, level of difficulty, vibration of the controller as it signals severity of movement, and user ID input. The final menu item is "Scores."

One can choose to be a number of male characters. The first time I played I chose to be a White, square-chinned wrestler named Briggs, who wears khakis and a dogtag. I fought against a White dude by the name of Spider. I was nearly flogged to death. The wrestling moves are clearly aimed to maim. It is said that rappers gave input to the game designers to come up with amazing moves. For example, the Ludacrisfication is "a bizzaro back-breaker in which he holds his victim prostrate, leaps into the air, then drives him into the ground with a knee in the back." (Buchanan, 2003: 25) Nevertheless, it was me (Briggs) against Spider, and he did me in. He rammed me head-first down into the floor where my neck must have surely snapped, and I would have died had this not been a video game. My total points: zilch! I had to figure out which buttons to push and when to push them and in what combinations. In any case, the next time, I still had the option to remain Briggs and I did (though I couldn't have lived through the brutality I experienced at the hands of Spider). This time, I fought a Black rapper named Proof. Again, I was brutalized. As I continued to try to learn to play the game, the next time I still remained Briggs and fought against a brutha named Tank. I was getting lucky, landing some good blows, but still in the end I was defeated. The announcer tried to revive me by telling me that I was "bringin shame to da game." And that I was "paid to fight." Instructions were flashing, telling me to "tap any button." I furiously tapped and pushed every button I could, but to no avail. Okay, I thought, "enough of being a White man, lemme try to be a brotha, and see if I can whoop some bootay." I chose to be Tank, the caramel-complexioned brotha with the blue backward baseball cap, sunglasses, and sexy goatee. As Tank, I am 5'10" and 242 lbs. By some strange combination of practice and trash talkin,[5] I whooped a White boy named Peewee's butt. I was hittin moves I didn't know I could make, the fistful of lead, the gritty slap. *Whatevuh.*

I must admit, it felt good when I was rewarded with a phat: "CONGRATULATIONS! Nice work! You unlocked Peewee in all game modes!" I began to win a little cash, $1,691, to be exact. I was now gettin into the groove. You know. I had to do it again. Next time I fought Drake, a guy who looked a lot like Briggs but dressed differently. Drake wears sunglasses, a white visor with two blue stripes, a neck chain, and Phat Farm overalls. I beat his butt and boosted my cash up to $10,588. I now had the option to "Develop," wherein you pay cash to upgrade your power. In this option I can increase my speed, grappling ability, stamina, and charisma (which was pretty low). However, the cost to "Develop" was $15,000 and I didn't have enough cash. I had no choice but to quit (exit, step off) or fight some more. I chose to fight, and Scarface was next. He immediately told me, "Now, you bout to get yo ass beat." And he did it. He beat my butt while wearin a suit. I gave him a little run for his money, though. Although I lost to Scarface I had at least won a couple of fights and I wanted to see if I would indeed be able to check out some honeys in the gallery. I still couldn't see any girls. The only way to unlock the photo gallery is to win girls in the "Story" mode. I thought if I were a "real" man, I would have to go to "Story" mode.

My point in sharing with you my experience of playing Def Jam Vendetta is not to give you a stream of consciousness narrative, but to give you (and myself) enough information upon which to base an analysis of sorts of how I am making meaning out of playing this video game. So I now turn to an application of Gee's concepts to my experience of Def Jam Vendetta.

Identification

Gee states that good video games capture players through appealing identities. Put another way, "Video games are 'rhetorically structured' to induce gamers to identify and act within the world of the video game in certain ways depending on the partisan interests with which a player-controlled agent or a gamer identifies." (Garrelts, 2003: 114) When I first played, I was a White man named Briggs. In a game depicting successful rappers as wrestlers, I figured the White wrestler would be an underdog in the underground because the whole global environment of the game drew on Hiphop ideology, which is accepted by Hiphoppas of all races but is understood as predominantly governed by Black aesthetics, and Briggs himself doesn't look Hiphop. He doesn't have the look that gives momentum from the git go, so to speak. He looks like a poor White male trying to survive in a tough world, where the odds are against him. One way to read the appeal of a Briggs is to focus on drive, skills, luck, and brute strength. In other words, this is a world where all that matters is how bad you want it or need it, your character, your skillz—not your color/race. This is a version of *8 Mile* (the Eminem story), where White boy outdoes Black men on their own turf, though some game industry insiders believe that "Gamers see great characters, not color." (Gwinn, 2004: 1) Certainly this is an idea that the White male gaming audience would buy into. Though the gaming industry gets input from Hiphoppas of color who are insiders, game designers are largely Whites and other non-Black people.[6] Wahneema Lubiano is not discussing video games and their racial assumptions, but his pronouncements on the idea of race and racism can be applied to this analysis. He says (1997: vii)

> [The ideas of race and racism] are the means by which a state and a political economy largely inimical to most of the U.S. citizenry achieve the consent of the governed. They act as a distorting prism that allows that citizenry to imagine itself functioning as a moral and just people while ignoring the widespread devastation directed at black Americans particularly, but at a much larger number of people generally.

Black designers and insiders fall prey to this racially careless thinking. It is a problem as it raises the issue of technological design. The characters in this game are one dimensional. They are just out to do whatever it takes to win. As stated in the liner notes, they are brutes—killing or at least maiming machines. Real-life wrestlers have brains, families, and dreams beyond checking out honeys and getting paid. Classism is reinforced through the one-dimensional representation of the White wrestling characters, while racism is reinforced through the limited presentation of the Black rappers and wrestlers. As one video-game critic asserts, "There is no way a game publisher would PROMOTE as of April 9, 2004, a 4.0 GPA Black athlete PROFILE in a computer console software game." (blacksoftware.com) While ingesting images of the one-dimensional lower-class White wrestler does not essentialize this one-dimensionality onto all White people in the minds of game players, historically, narrowcasting of Black images has the effect of essentializing Black people. As Adam Banks (2006) has argued, design is rhetorical. Blacks have been designed into positions of exclusion. While all of this is certainly within the constellation of me playing this game, I get caught up in wanting to land a drop kick. I want to win, but I lose badly as Briggs, a couple of times. So I switch gears and become a new character, a brutha, Tank. I was immediately attracted to Tank because he does have the look—the backward baseball cap, sunglasses, and sexy goatee. In the world of this game, it is to one's advantage to think like or to become a heterosexist male, as gender and sexuality role playing is central to the game's ethos. I would go through any agony to reach a higher level to check out the fly honeys!

Interaction

In good video games words and deeds are contextualized from within their interactive environment. This game is about getting to the top of the fight game, gaining the most money, power, and rewards that this life has to offer. The first time I won, I felt good. I wanted to keep winning and earning more money. As soon as I reached a certain level of success I was offered the opportunity to "Develop," to pay money to be more powerful and strong. The game is a world unto itself. You and the character you are playing want to win. Once you engage the game, winning is all that matters. It is for this reason that when you reach a certain level you can buy more power. It's the video-game equivalent of athletes taking steroids to ensure their competitive edge. Win at all costs. As a culture, we don't admit to this principle openly, but our societal structure and history bear out the fact that our disposition toward winning is an unwritten value of American culture.

Def Jam Vendetta incorporates the values of the dominant society as well as opposing, marginalized values, as should be the case since it incorporates Hiphop aesthetics. As in the larger society, as a game simulating mainstream/dominant ideology, it is a decidedly male-gendered game. The embedded narratives and the root narrative as well as the game environment—images, voices, styles—are all male centered. As in commercial Hiphop, with few exceptions, females are in the background, they are "eye candy" for the males, a part of the male reward system for being masculine (you get to check out honeys if you achieve enough). This is one of the defining characteristics of commercial Hiphop and of Def Jam Vendetta as a Hiphop video game. "That's just how the Game go," as one of my students put it. What my student referred to as the Game is actually "Any entity or endeavor involving established practices and ways of doing something—The Academic Game, the Rap Game . . . [etc.]" (Smitherman, 2006) In this case, it's the Rap Game, and to a large extent the Video Game industry.

An aspect of Def Jam Vendetta's interaction that at first puzzled me is the lack of verbal assault on the part of the simulated rappers. Real bruthas will beat you literally and verbally, simultaneously. And this reminded me of the artificiality of the game. However, some game industry insiders stress that Hiphop video games help players feel closer to the culture. (Marshall, 2005: 60[7]) For example, in Def Jam Fight for New York, a sequel to Def Jam Vendetta, players can design their players and even have diamonds made by the jeweler to rap stars, Jacob. As I reflected on the lack of verbal dueling, I realized that perhaps the reason why player-controlled game agents don't do a lot of talking is so that the songs remain audible and integral to the action of the scenes. Further, I noticed that my voice began to engage the game. I was the one talkin more trash than a little bit. In this way the player of the game begins to merge with the game world. My language and knowledge of how to empower myself help me to empower my player-controlled agent/wrestler.

Producer

As an engaged player of the game, I am co-creator of the text. Now this part is tricky because there is the issue of structure and agency. As demonstrated by Garrelts (2003), although the game is structured by choices, it has a rhetoric and a grammar. The motivation to win or fully explore the game keeps the player making choices that hopefully will prove successful. For example, when I began winning fights and acquiring cash, I wanted to continue my success. I could not make new rules or attitudes for the game, though. My choices are to quit or continue to fight. The game is structured that way. My choices are undergirded by the capitalist system of the game—buy more strength, or work to be able to purchase it. "Like the worker who needs to work to survive and is given incentive enough to maintain his/her existence, so is the player-controlled agent given enough incentive to consume" (Garrelts. 2003: 129), or to continue fighting, as it were. These "choices" mirror the complex position of rappers. As the music industry exploits and promotes verbal battles, beefs, and survival of the fittest (sometimes to the death of rappers), gamers draw on this "ride or die" sociocultural orientation from the world of commercial Hiphop.

Agency

How does agency figure in a game such as Def Jam Vendetta? As game players are making choices about the game and experiencing what it has to offer, players do achieve a sense of agency. I know I did. I can control my player-controlled agent; however, I cannot change the rhetoric of the game. I cannot have my player-controlled agent/wrestler grow tired of breaking backs and necks. I cannot direct my wrestler to dread that he and his opponents have to face death just to make a living. It is for this reason that one game theorist, Gonzalo Frasca (2004), argues that video games should be designed so that players can explore complex societal problems which encourage gamers to question the values and assumptions of the games.[8]

What I have tried to show here is that Hiphop video-game players are drawing on their knowledge of how the real world works when they become engaged players of a game. Hiphop video games, like other popular media, are sites of competing discourses, symbolizing ideologies, and worldviews. As we take on identities offered by the game, we are able to view the world from a different perspective, which is not a bad thing. Gamers are making choices, but as most of these games are currently designed, the type of agency available does not induce gamers to think critically about the world of the game. Garrelts (2003) argues that many game scholars see the game user as easily duped and being controlled by the game. He does not agree with this position. Neither do I, but at the same time, I do see that Hiphop video games are not designed to challenge certain "commonsense" assumptions about societal groups and Black youth culture in particular. I think it is very important for educators to bring video games into their curricula as a tool for exploring what it is that we know about society, how games ask us to apply this knowledge, and if there is anything we can do to change things.

APPENDIX

Shared vocabulary

Hiphop words/phrases

EXAMPLE	DEFINITION	ARTIST(S)	SONG
get wid it **bad** gal nuh waan nuh one minute	bad—so good it has to be bad. (See Smitherman, 1977/1986: 44.) Similar to Jamaican "wicked."	Sean Paul feat. Cecile	Can You Do the Work
Like a **balla** wi a go dung di franc	balla—reference to a ladies' man or one who makes large sums of money, drug dealer (Smitherman, 2000)	Elephant Man	Pon De River
Remind me of the **benz**, the lexus, the **bimmer** and if a boy call u **bitch** gal a no nuh nuttin	benz—the Mercedes Benz car; bimmer—BMW car bitch—a generic term for a female; some women do not appreciate it (Smitherman, 2000: 69)	Bounty Killa Vybz Kartel	Benz and Bimmer mixtape
See wi diamon ring . . . cashflow **bling bling**	bling bling—coined in 1999 in "Bling-Bling" by B.G. of the Big Tymers and Hot Boys. References the blinding shine of sparkly jewelry, diamonds, consumer/commodity culture of the contemporary global society.	Spragga Benz	U Suppose to Know
Blunt dem so big a mus fi Bunny, Bob, and Peter	blunt—marijuana cigar	Jr. Gong Marley (Stephen Marley, Redman, Method Man)	Lyrical 44

EXAMPLE	DEFINITION	ARTIST(S)	SONG
Bomb she bomb	bomb—excellent	Buju Banton	Di Woman Dem Phat
Boogie down pon di dance floor	boogie down—"to party" (Smitherman, 2000: 76)	Beenie Man	Boogie Down
Nobody nuh fih know seh Shaggy a **bone** it	bone—the sex act from the male point of view or the penis itself (Smitherman, 2000)	Shaggy	Hot Gal
You're not my **boo**	boo—significant other (Smitherman, 2000)	T.O.K.	Last Night
Last night I made a **booty call**	booty call—a phone call to a potential sexual partner mainly for the purpose of arranging sexual intercourse	Wayne Wonder	Keep Dem Coming
Gimmi di **chicken head** dem	chicken head—"dumb female" (Smitherman, 2000: 90)	Vybz Kartel	Sweet to Di Belly
We used to **chill** down in a di shack	chill—"to relax." (Smitherman, 2000: 91)	Roundhead	High Everyday
Well a man bun up de **chronic**	chronic—strong marijuana	Mr. Vegas and Sean Paul	Hot Gyal Today
I'm **clockin** all the honies	clockin—to watch (Smitherman, 2000); honies—generic reference for a female (positive) (Smitherman, 2000)	Baby Cham and Alias	Holiday
my **crew** my **dogs** set rules . . . **represent** for di lord of yaads	crew—main unit of social, economic, and emotional support in Hiphop (Morgan, 2001); dogs—male term of endearment; represent— "to exemplify a group, position, cultural style . . . a model example of the group or thing being represented" (Smitherman, 2000: 245)	T.O.K	Chichi Man

EXAMPLE	DEFINITION	ARTIST(S)	SONG
what the **dealio**?	dealio—with an added flair, "what the dealio?" is an alternate way of asking "what is going on?" or "what's the deal,"	Wayne Wonder	Keep Dem Coming
No bwoy caan **diss** mi	dis[s]—show disrespect (Smitherman, 2000)	Tanto Metro	No Bwoy
dat nigga dat ya wan break **dough** wit/dat dude dat **dude**	dough—money dude—generic reference for a male (Smitherman, 2000)	Fras Krew	Dat Dude
pass the **dro**/bus anotha bokkle o **moe** . . . But you no let them **sweat ya**	dro—strong marijuana moe—moet, a brand of champagne; sweat—"to bother or hassle someone" (Smitherman, 2000: 274)	Sean Paul	Gimme the Light
wait until Def Jamaica **drops**	drop—inform or explain; or release a CD. (Smitherman, 2000) Reference to Def Jam label's ability to distribute Dancehallas more widely and the DJ's diffusion of knowledge in U.S. and abroad.	Wayne Marshall (Dipset, Vybz Kartel)	Straight off the top
So everybody can understand my **flow**	flow—the way that a rapper solidifies his/her vocals rhythmically and sonically within the track or the beat	Baby Cham and Alias	Holiday
Gangsta na lef dem guns from me roun it	gangsta—a person or thing representing rebellion against societal standards (Smitherman, 2000: 142)	Sizzla	mixtape
Imagine you dress up inna your latest **gear**	gear—clothes (Smitherman, 2000)	Beenie Man	We a Star
Quick to grab de **gat**	gat—"a gun" (Smitherman, 2000: 143)	T.O.K.	War
Get Busy/Get jiggy/**get crunked** up **perculate**	get busy—"to start to do something—to party, talk work etc" (Smitherman, 2000: 146); get crunked—"high energy, a party atmosphere." Word developed out of US Southern rap club music	Sean Paul	Get Busy

EXAMPLE	DEFINITION	ARTIST(S)	SONG
	culture. (*Slanguistics*, 2004); perculate—a dance		
Now reggae and **Hiphop** hand and hand . . . **benjamins** crazy **props**	Hiphop—the culture which spawned rap and other elements in 1970s Bronx, New York; benjamins—$100 bills or money in general (Smitherman, 2000); props—respect or recognition (Smitherman, 2000)	Vybz Kartel (Wayne Marshall, Dipset)	Straight off the Top
then we know she's a **hoe**	ho[e]—AAL pronunciation for whore. Still controversial though some women use it intimately among themselves. (Smitherman, 2000)	Mr. Vegas	She's a Hoe
Ain't no **homie** gone play me	homie—"a person from one's neighborhood" (Smitherman, 2000: 168)	Ini Kamoze	Here Come the Hotstepper
She loves da **hood** . . . shorty sleep at my **crib** . . .	hood—shortened form of (ghetto) neighborhood. In Jamaican Dancehall slang wood and hood refer to the penis, thus Baby Cham is playing off both senses; crib—one's home (Smitherman, 2000)	Baby Cham	The Hood
Hype up and kick up	hype—"doing something excellently or superbly" (Smitherman, 2000: 105)	Lady Saw	Eh Em Eh Em
A buss the platinum wrist wid all a finger full a **ice**	ice—diamonds	Ward 21	Haters
keepin it **jiggy**	jiggy—someone/something superb (Smitherman, 2000); "rich, lots of money" (*Slanguistics*, 2004)	Elephant Man	Keepin it Jiggy
ol school **kicks** . . . cap an **do rag** no Akademics	kicks—shoes (Smitherman, 2000) do rag—"a scarf, handkerchief, or stocking cap . . . used to preserve [one's] do. The term	Vybz Kartel	Stunt 101 [50 Cent track]/ Jersey mix

EXAMPLE	DEFINITION	ARTIST(S)	SONG
	originated in the era when dos, processes, and conks were stylish." Also gang head rag. (Smitherman, 2000, 110)		
From the contrac right and the dollas **legit**	legit—"refers to anything that's authentic; real, not fake; describes something that's appropriate, in order" (Smitherman, 2000: 191)	Bounty Killa	Tempt Mi
Makaveli/Shelly belly	Makaveli—a persona created by renowned slain rapper Tupac on his CD *Makaveli: The Don Killuminati (The 7 Day Theory)*, influenced by Machiavelli's *The Prince*. It was alleged that Tupac would disappear and that this CD would regenerate intense interest in his music. Elephant's use suggests that his own music regenerates interest in Dancehall.	Elephant Man	Dance Di Crazy Hype
I'm de daddy of the **mack daddies**	mack daddy—"a man who has a lot of women and plays them" (Smitherman, 2000: 197)	Ini Kamoze	Here Come the Hotstepper
have **madd** fun . . . ina farin **madd** people a fly dung	madd—a quantifier, a lot, huge amount; crazy or extreme (Morgan, 2001: 203)	Elephant Man	Mad Instruments
Just to lose my **main squeeze**	main squeeze—"lover, favorite girlfriend" (Major, 1970/1994: 296)	Beenie Man	Who Am I?
I don't give a damn I'm the real **mamma jamma**	mamma jamma—"Euphemism for muthafucka" (Smitherman, 2000: 198)	Lady Saw	Dancehall Queen
Put your **muddafuckin** hands in di air	muddafuckin—Jamaican pronunciation of muthafucka—"Used to refer to a person, place or thing, either negatively or postively, depending on context"	T.O.K.	Hands in the Air

EXAMPLE	DEFINITION	ARTIST(S)	SONG
	(Smitherman, 1994: 164)—an intensifer.		
Who ya callin **nigga**	nigga—term in existence from seventeenth century for Jamaicans. Contemporarily it is not used as liberally there as among U.S. Blacks. Among both groups the term can have negative, neutral, or endearing reference; generally Blacks of both groups would not appreciate usage by Whites. (Cassidy and Le Page, 2002; Smitherman, 2000)	Capleton	Who Ya Callin Nigga?
buck up ina **o.p.p.**	o.p.p.—"other people's [sexual] property" (Smitherman, 2000: 221)	Sean Paul	Safe Sex
Nah support no bwoy, wah bruk we foot and tek we **paper**	paper—money (Smitherman, 2000) (when someone bruk ya foot, they've let you down, caused you an undue burden, usually financially)	Elephant Man	Nah Gwaan a Jamaica
Dem a **playahate** but me	playahate—an envious person, one who expresses extreme dislike for another's success in any life endeavor (Smitherman, 2000)	Vybz Kartel	mixtape
You getting paid not **played**/**Pushin** Escalade and **rockin** prada . . .	played—to be outsmarted (Smitherman, 2000); pushin—driving a car (Major, 1970/1994); rockin—to wear clothing with style	Buju Banton	Paid Not Played
We **roll** wit two **glock**/From Portmore to **New Jack**	roll—to associate with, ride in a car (Smitherman, 2000); glock—powerful handgun (Smitherman, 2000); New Jack—new urban Hiphop culture (Smitherman, 2000)	Vybz Kartel	More Life
Mi and **Shorty** rollin wid di Glock 40/Badman party: **fly** crazy	shorty—a generic reference for a female (Smitherman, 2000);	Vybz Kartel	Badman Party

110

EXAMPLE	DEFINITION	ARTIST(S)	SONG
	fly—"exciting, dazzling, upscale, in the know" (Smitherman, 2000: 133)		
Welcome to Jamrock/ Camp weh di **tugs** dem camp at	thug—[tug, Jamaican pronunciation], "Someone who has gone through a lot of hardship in one's life, meaning becoming a thug, you don't have any money so you make money by any means necessary. Livin' life thug style" (http://www. rapdict.org/Thug)	Damian "Jr. Gong" Marley	Welcome to Jamrock
Dem style dey **wack**	wack—undesirable (Smitherman, 2000)	Lady Saw	Eh Em Eh Em
Dash weh di CD when me bun **weed**	weed—marijuana (Smitherman, 2000)	Vybz Kartel	'Ganja Burs' (?—title of tune unknown)
Hol up wait a minute/let me **break it down** slow	break it down—"to explain something" (Smitherman, 2000: 81)	Baby Cham and Alias	Holiday
they **got it goin on**	got it goin on—"superbly or effectively doing something" (Smitherman, 2000: 153)	Shaggy	Hey Sexy Lady
Don't **hate da playa**/just hate the **game**	Don't hate da playa—phrase originating in street entreprenuerism. Playas work various games—the girl game, the trick game, the dope game, etc. The practices of the game maximize profit and from a non-playa's perspective gives the playa an unfair advantage. Hence, the imperative.	Beenie Man	Don't Hate
Keepin it real doin the music for the fans	keepin it real—phrase suggesting a commitment to authenticity and honesty	Elephant Man	Pon De River
Shizzle my nizzle	shizzle my nizzle—may be out of the Bay Area, popularized by Snoop Dogg. Adding the suffix "-izzle" to various words. Done in	Elephant Man	Online

EXAMPLE	DEFINITION	ARTIST(S)	SONG
	"Double Dutch Bus" by Frankie Smith. (http://www.nationmaster.com/encyclopedia/Hip-hop-slang)		

Dancehall words/phrases

EXAMPLE	DEFINITION	ARTIST(S)	SONG
for sure mi **a go** do it	a go—"Preceeding another verb, this forms phrases expressing the future." (Cassidy and Le Page, 2002: 6)	A Tribe Called Quest	The Chase
After a good plate of some **ackee and saltfish**	ackee and saltfish—Jamaica's national dish consisting of ackee, a type of fruit, codfish, onions, peppers and seasoning; usually eaten for breakfast	CamRon of Dipset (Vybz Kartel, Wayne Marshall)	Straight off the Top
till they reach **Babylon** behold the psychic phenomenon	Babylon—people and institutions carrying out the objectives of colonialism and its legacies which have oppressed African peoples since the seventeenth century. (Edmonds, 1998: 23) "A biblical allusion often made by the Rastafari, hence, from their point of view, non-believers, white men." (Cassidy and Le Page, 2002: 17)	Killah Priest	B.I.B.L.E.
a shotty boy poppin at you **batty boys**	batty boys—batty or bati refers to the buttocks. A battyboy is a homosexual male. Cassidy and Le Page (2002) also indicate pederast —one who prefers anal sex with boys.	CamRon of Dipset (Vybz Kartel, Wayne Marshall)	Straight Off The Top
move from in front mi with your **bati fies** (face)	bati (fies)—"The buttocks; common among schoolboys and generally in the vulgar	A Tribe Called Quest	Eight Million Stories

EXAMPLE	DEFINITION	ARTIST(S)	SONG
	phrase /yu bati/ expressing anger, disdain, or general insult." (Cassidy and Le Page, 2002: 32)		
Backshots keep a nigga open	backshot—sexual position where, in heterosexual sex, the man enters the woman's vagina from behind her rather than facing her.	Nas	Pussy Kills
Now tha baby's in the trash heap **bawlin**	bawl—"much more commonly used in Jamaica than in England or the U.S. . . . To wail, cry, weep." (Cassidy and Le Page, 2002: 33)	Tupac	Brenda's Got a Baby
A **beef patty** and some **coco bread**.	beef patty—a baked turnover filled with Jamaican seasoned cooked ground beef, an English influenced food, an island hamburger of sorts—but far more tasty (http://www.jamaicans.com/tourist/overview/eating-2.shtml); coco bread—a flaky soft pleasant-tasting bread/roll of Jamaica	Lauryn Hill	Every Ghetto Every City
like a warning shot **blocka blocka**	blocka blocka—onomatopoeic representation for the sound of gunshots; done to show enjoyment of a performance	Foxy Brown feat. Sizzla	Come Fly with Me
Booyacka booyacka off a Jimmy **Rankin**	booyaka booyaka—onomatopoeic representation for the sound of gunshots; done to show enjoyment of a performance; Rankin—"person of significant power . . . in a poor or ghetto community" (Patrick, 1995: 251)	Jim Jones of Dipset (Vybz Kartel, Wayne Marshall)	Straight off the Top
with my **bredren** from reflection	bredren—preferred Jamaican for brethren; fellow male Rastas (http:	Mos Def (Talib Kweli, DJ Hi Tek)	This Means You

113

EXAMPLE	DEFINITION	ARTIST(S)	SONG
	//www.ibpc.fr/~dror/ rastadror.html); "male friend holding same beliefs as the speaker" (Pollard, 2000: 41)		
No **chichi** niggas allowed	chi chi—a homosexual. As chichi is identified in Cassidy and Le Page (2002) as perhaps from an African language meaning small and in Jamaican as a dry wood termite; and because wood or hood is a slang term for penis, Cooper (2004: 163) suggests that chichi means a diminutive or vulnerable man.	Busta Rhymes	Everybody Rise Again
Went from **baldheaded** to all **dreaded**	baldhead—"person not dealing with Rasta . . . person who has not got his hair in locks" (Pollard, 2000: 41); dread—"Rasta" (Pollard, 2000: 42); dread(locks)—"loose, thick braids" (Smitherman, 2000: 117)	Nappy Roots	Blowin Trees
One **dreadlock** is stronger than one strand	dreadlock—see "dread" above	Dead Prez	Psychology
Lick shots, work ya seat up	lick shot—"firing a gun or imitating its sound (done at the Dancehall as a mark of respect for the performing artiste)" (Francis-Jackson, 2002: 31)	Notorious B.I.G.	Long Kiss Goodnight
Licks, Licks, boy on your **baxside**	lick—"This word is far more commonly used in Jamaica than in Britain or U.S. in these senses—more than hit, strike, or other synonyms" (Cassidy and Le Page, 2002: 273); backside—"the posterior or rump" (Oxford English Dictionary); this word appears to be used in this	A Tribe Called Quest	Oh My God

114

EXAMPLE	DEFINITION	ARTIST(S)	SONG
	sense more among Jamaicans than African Americans		
The doctor said I had **Bloodclots**	bloodclot—cuss word, literally, a sanitary napkin (See Cassidy and Le Page, 2002, "bloodcloth.")	Kanye West	Through the Wire
big up the east coast and the west	big up—"phrase used to pay homage, to compliment a person, group, locale, business. Often used in shout outs." (Smitherman, 2000: 68) Smitherman doesn't speculate the origins of the phrase. My sources indicate that it is a Jamaican creation.	KRS-One	Throw Down
Busta Rhymes cookin up a little **brown stew chicken**	brown stew chicken—a tasty Jamaican meal prepared with a selection of chicken, spices, onions, escallions, tomato, carrot, potato, and browning. Busta Rhymes implies that his rhymes are as flavorful.	Busta Rhymes	Holla
motherfuckin **buckshots**	buckshots—voiced to show approval, alludes to gunshot salute—rapper implies that his rhymes are so excellent and hot that they themselves are loud/extreme gunshots (buckshots)	Ice Cube	Anybody Seen The PoPos
And there he was this young **bwoy** a stranger to my eyes	bwoy (bwaai/boy)—"This pronunc[iation] is still very common among [Jamaican] speakers" (Cassidy and Le Page, 2002: 86)	Fugees	Killing Me Softly
Check for a nigga check for a nigga	check—"call upon, visit someone (often with a request" (Patrick, 1995: 238)	Capadonna	Check for a Nigga
fresh vegetable with **ital** stew/sweet yam fries with the green **callaloo**	ital—"Rastafarian food . . . prepared in a special (and natural) way" (Pollard, 2000: 14); callaloo—"The name given	Dead Prez	Be Healthy

EXAMPLE	DEFINITION	ARTIST(S)	SONG
	to several plants having edible leaves, eaten as greens" (Cassidy and Le Page, 2002: 89, "Calalu")		
The original **don dada** nobody bomb harda	don dada—"the highest of Dons" (http://www.ibpc.fr/ ~dror/rastadror.html) Patrick (1995) speculates that the usage of "don"(from Italian) in Jamaica may have preceded *The Godfather* (the movie that popularized the term).	50 Cent feat. Tony Yayo	Like My Style
if a thing tes me run **fi** me gun	fe(fi)—"possessive particle . . . preceding a pronoun, or occasionally a person's name" (Cassidy and Le Page, 2002: 176)	Lauryn Hill	Lost Ones
puffin **ganja** get to your crib can't find her	ganja—"weed of wisdom" associated with the beliefs and faith of Rastafari (Pollard, 1986: 161)	Nas and Foxy Brown	Watch Dem Niggas
I **gwaan** murder dem	gwaan—"alternates with **a go** to show 'progressive' present tense or future tense" (Cassidy and Le Page, 2002: 217)	Foxy Brown feat. Sizzla	Come Fly with Me
Jamaica posse most high **Haile Selassie** . . . another **Sound boy** killin	Haile Selassie—Ras Tafari was crowned in 1930 as the Ethiopian Emperor of Addis Ababa, Haile Selassie I, known in the Rastafarian faith as the conquering lion of the tribe of Judah, the saviour; Sound boy—the sound system consists of a selector who plays records via a turntable, with huge amplified speakers, and other technology. Persons employed as to work the Sound via DJing, or otherwise operating the Sound, are Sound boys. To kill the sound	Method Man (Redman, Jr. Gong and Stephen Marley)	Lyrical 44

116

EXAMPLE	DEFINITION	ARTIST(S)	SONG
	boy is to outperform him by audience approval.		
My **posse inna** Brooklyn wear the mask	posse—Patrick (1995: 251) asserts that this term has spread to AAVE usage in the sense of crew "one's associates etc."; inna—"a common variant of iin: in, to, into" (Cassidy and Le Page, 2002: 234)	Fugees	The Mask
Jah lick dem	Jah—Rastafarian word for Jehovah in Rastafarian religion and culture. (Cassidy and Le Page, 2002: 240)	A Tribe Called Quest	Oh My God
You **a-fi** listen a **likkle**	a-fi/haffi—preferred Jamaican, where Standard uses "have to"; likkle—preferred Jamaican pronunciation for "little"	Queen Latifah	Nuff of the Ruff Stuff
Don't even ask, whole a dem a **mash up** . . .	mash up—"Beat, break, smash, crush; the sense passing into spoil, destroy" (Cassidy and Le Page, 2002: 296)	Foxy Brown feat. Sizzla	Come Fly with Me
I'm in Jamaica spendin **massive** bucks while the ladies all beggin me to **mash it up**	massive—"DJ term for people in a party . . . perhaps a folk etymological amelioration of the somewhat pejorative 'masses'" (Cooper, 1995: 171); mash it up—"an expression of encouragement" (Francis-Jackson, 2002: 33)	Ludacris	Pimpin All Over The World
Hollerin Beenie Mon, see me **mon**	mon—"a fellow, friend: used by and of members of either sex in situations of informal or familiar conversation" (Cassidy and Le Page, 2002: 290)	Nelly	Country Grammar
Murderation modern hangin education . . .	muderation (murdah)—"an expression to describe something eye-catching or	Dead Prez	Assassination

EXAMPLE	DEFINITION	ARTIST(S)	SONG
	great, a wicked piece of music, etc." (Francis-Jackson, 2002: 35)		
Bad **gyal nah** fi pose	gyal—Jamaican pronunciation for gal, a female; nah—"Not, followed by a progressive tense of a verb" (Cassidy and Le Page, 2002: 314)	Lil' Kim (Beenie Man)	Fresh from Yaad
I'm a queen, **nuff respect**	nuff respect—nuff is the preferred Jamaican for enough, meaning plentiful (Cassidy and Le Page, 2002). Nuff respect is a greeting given to someone worthy of admiration. A parallel of giving props.	Queen Latifah	Fly Girl
If a thing tes **me** run fe **me** gun	me/mi—"The first personal pronoun singular, without distinction of case: I, me, my" (Cassidy and Le Page, 2002: 298).	Lauryn Hill	Lost Ones
ovastan somethin	ovastan—coming into Jamaican through Rastafarian Dread Talk. "Used for understand, for if you are in control of an idea, you must stand over it." (Pollard, 2000: 10)	Joe Budden	Ma Ma Ma
Hey, **posse**'s in effect	posse—Smitherman (2000) indicates a network of friends and associates, similar to crew. Patrick (1995) indicates that this sense spread to AAVE from Jamaican. I think the Westerns play a large role in the use of this sense of the term among AAVE speakers.	Public Enemy	Bring Tha Noise
Six for the **politrix** Seven call the Reverend	politrix—a Rastafarian innovation in the language which reflects the Rastafarian distrust of Babylonian representatives. (See Pollard,	Goapele	The Daze

EXAMPLE	DEFINITION	ARTIST(S)	SONG
	1986: 160 for explanation of Category II)		
Wish death **pon** me . . .	pon—preferred Jamaican for "upon" (see "pan" in Cassidy and Le Page, 2002)	50 Cent	Many Men (Wish Death)
nigga be drunk off **punnani**	punnani—vagina (Cooper, 2004: 244)	Prodigy (Lil' Kim featuring Mobb Deep and Mr. Cheeks)	Jumpoff Remix
Packin like a **rasta** in the weed spot	rasta—a member of the Rastafarian faith of either gender, but the usage in this example may refer to a male	Nas	It Ain't Hard To Tell
Buffalo Soldier **Rastafari** style	Rastafari—a faith and way of life that views Haile Selassie I as God; they seek repatriation to Africa; they believe in self-reliance, reasoning, clean eating and living, and adhere to many of the principles asserted by Marcus Garvey, Alexander Bedward, and other early leaders	Beanie Sigel feat. Bun B	Purple Rain
Rastaman toss me pounds	Rastaman—a male member of the Rastafarian faith	50 Cent with Young Buck, Lloyd Banks, Lil Flip	P.I.M.P. Remix (Big Mike mixtape)
Where youth and policeman they nah **reach** agreement	reach/riich—"to arrive at" (Cassidy and Le Page, 2002: 376)	Mos Def (Talib Kweli and DJ Hi Tek)	This Means You
boy for now just **sekkle**	sekkle—Jamaican pronunciation for "settle"	KRS-One	My Philosophy
Selecta come!!!!!	-selecta—"the non performing DJ who selects records, operates turntables, and plays records" (Francis-Jackson, 2002: 47)	Redman (Method Man, Jr. Gong, and Stephen Marley)	Lyrical 44
We the movie **shottas**/but it's really **rude bois**	shotta—perhaps influenced by the term "big shot," someone known to use or	CamRon	Leave Me Alone Pt. 2

EXAMPLE	DEFINITION	ARTIST(S)	SONG
	carry guns/gunman/a participant in organized crime; rude bois/bwoys—young males at odds with societal values and the received social order; outlaws. Originally emerging in 1960s Kingston, Jamaica, and beginning in the 1970s to be influenced by poverty and politicians, rude boys began to control areas of Jamaica with violence. Currently, rude boy does not necessarily imply involvement in organized crime.		
If you got a **spliff** then put it in the air	spliff—a ganja cigarette. The word is said to derive from US slang "splifficate" —to make drunk. (Cassidy and Le Page, 2002: 420)	Talib Kweli	Put it in the Air
try to **tief** off my piece	tief—"Sneak; act in a furtive or surreptitious manner" (Patrick, 1995: 257); to steal	Lauryn Hill	Forgive Them Father
I give you every bloodclaat **ting**	ting—Jamaican pronunciation of "thing."	Twista (Elephant Man, Youngbloodz, Kiprich)	Jook Gal Remix
when it come to other rappers . . . boy get **vex**	vex—"to affect with a feeling of dissatisfaction, annoyance, or irritation; to cause (one) to fret, grieve, or feel unhappy." (*Oxford English Dictionary*)	Missy Elliott	On & On
whole a dem a mash up . . .	whole a dem—preferred Jamaican for "all of them."	Foxy Brown feat. Sizzla)	Come Fly With Me
on my **wicked** high gotta have that dank	wicked—a positive evaluator meaning extraordinary, excellent	Three Six Mafia	Sippin on Some Syrup
wine just like a **reggae** tune	wine (wain, whine, win)—dance that features gyration of the hips in a seductive manner;	Busta Rhymes	We Got What You Want

EXAMPLE	DEFINITION	ARTIST(S)	SONG
	reggae—"The 1967 *Dictionary of Jamaican English* defines 'reggae' as 'a recently estab[lished] sp[elling] for rege (the basic sense of which is *ragged*—see *rege rege* with possible ref[erence] to rag-time music (an early form of American jazz) but referring esp[ecially] to the slum origins of this music in Kingston" (Cooper, 2004: 236)		
Them belly full my trigger finger got pulled	them belly full—one source cites "Rain a fall, but de dutty tough. Me belly full but me hungry" (Watson, 1991: 214) as the proverb. Another cites "When belly full, jaw must stop." (Prahlad, 2001: 239) Proverb indicates the paradox of needs and wants. In Bob Marley's song "Dem Belly Full" on the *Natty Dread* album, Marley sings, "Them belly full but we hungry," indicating oppressive life conditions for poor Jamaicans.	Dead Prez	Assassination

Common Hiphop/Dancehall words/phrases

EXAMPLE	DEFINITION	ARTIST(S)	SONG
Babymama or Babymother/It's my **babymama** (ye ain' know?)	babymama—(African American context) "[term] emerged as a label for irresponsible [unmarried] mothers who are thus . . . insignificant." (Smitherman, 2000: 59) Over time, the term can be used neutrally or to show esteem as in Fantasia's (2004) song of that title.	Three Six Mafia	Babymama

EXAMPLE	DEFINITION	ARTIST(S)	SONG
Babymadda/babymother . . . Das all mi baby madda, she waan war wi	babymother—(Jamaican context) "Woman who is carrying or has given birth to a man's child, but is not married to the man." (Patrick, 1995: 232–3) Patrick shows attestation from 1989 Jamaica Gleaner.	Harry Toddler	Bare Gal
I ain't that **baby's daddy** . . .	babydaddy—(African American context)—see "babymother" but apply to child's father	Wyclef Jean	Babydaddy
Mi carry it come and nyam it wit mi **baby fadda**	baby fadda—(Jamaican context) "man who fathers a child, but is not married to the mother (co-habitation and common-law marriage not implied)." (Patrick, 1995: 232) Patrick's attestation is from Sistren Theatre 1987.	Macka Diamond	Tek Con
spittin that drama/But when I **bus** they say hush; And **bus** a extra whine and mek we seed up a son	bus—West African-influenced phonology (no consonant pairs); to perform, as in to create a rhyme, a song, or a dance move; also, to reveal	Mia X (Da Crime Family); Tanya Stephens	Buss That; It's a Pity
do dat dance/Pretty lady go on do dat dance;I'm dat nigga dat you really wan roll wit	dat (that)—West African-influenced phonology (no th) demonstrative—that particular one, a deictic expression	Baby a.k.a. #1 Stunna; Fras Krew	Dat Dude; Do That
Where **dem** dollas at nigga; When **dem** gal deh a wine she like mumma killa; We like **dem** boyz that be in nem lac's leanin; Nuff a **dem** a freak . . . Thug nigga wanna bees nuff a **dem** a lick it back	dem—West African-influenced phonology (no th sound); demonstrative	Gangsta Boo; Beenie Man; Destiny's Child; T.O.K.	Where Dem Dollas At; Dancehall Queen; Soldier; ChiChi Man
Yo, who **dis**?; Some body ago get mash up **dis** evening	dis (this)—West African-influenced phonology (no th), a demonstrative, a deictic expression	The Roots/ feat. Ursula Rucker; Mr. Vegas	The Unlocking; Unda Mi Guinness

EXAMPLE	DEFINITION	ARTIST(S)	SONG
Knuck if you buck **boy**	boy—a young male. There is no indication that the rappers intend to invoke Jamaican; however, the pronunciation is identical with Jamaican. In American English the vowel sound is long oi, as [oi]; in Jamaican it is pronounced like long I, so that boy rhymes with "tie." It is represented in spelling with a w, as in "bwai."	Crime Mob	Knuck if You Buck
Lord have mercy/Laad a mercy **Lord have mercy**! If the broad is thirsty/I'll have her man reimburse me; The gal sey dem need a good plumber/**Laad have mercy** and dem should know well	Lord/Laad have mercy—Sacred/Secular. Commonplace saying among Blacks in the United States and Jamaica. The phrase reflects the African worldview and diasporic practice which recognizes the inextricability of the spiritual from the material or the sacred from the secular.	LL Cool J; Bounty Killa	HeadSprung; Benz and Bimmer
these **pickaninnies** get wit anything to sell records	pickaninnies—Major (1970/1994) identifies pickaninny/pickney as an African word for child that came into use in the old slave states. The Jamaican word is pickney. Cassidy and Le Page (2002) explain that the word developed from Spanish "Pequenos Ninnos," meaning young children. The term came into Portuguese and African pidgin Englishes such as those in Cameroon and Sierra Leone as "pickny," and Barbados, Belize, Guyana	Nas	These Are Our Heroes
waitin for **wifey** to leave	wifey—woman in a serious relationship with a man (Smitherman, 2006)	Busta Rhymes	Wife in Law
That's what the fuck it is **nuff said**	Jamaican pronunciation of "enough said."	Xzibit feat. Busta Rhymes	Tough Guy

NOTES

1 Black/folk/discoursez

1 Japan, New Zealand, Bosnia, Italy, Spain, France, Germany, South Africa, Canada, and Hawaii are examples. For more see Mitchell, 2001.

2 See Crawford, 2001, in which chapters by Nehusi, Blackshire-Belay, and Ernie Smith are very informative on the Africologist perspective. They argue, for example, that Ebonics are new African languages.

3 Although Dalby's explanation seems pretty straightforward, scholars haven't settled the matter of whether Ebonic languages are European languages that should be categorized as members of the Indo-European language family or if they are newly created African languages that should be categorized as Niger–Kordofanian derived languages. It appears that part of the problem of definition for scholars of language is ideological and paradigmatic. For example, in the case of US Ebonics, Blackshire-Belay (1996) points to the problem that scholars use traditional racist terminology and paradigms in discussing the speech of peoples of African descent. This tradition is inadequate as these paradigms were created to justify the social and political domination and oppression of peoples of African descent and so traditional terminology must be rejected. Schools of thought on the origins and development of US Ebonics can be divided into at least three categories: Dialectologist (also called Anglicist), Creolist, and Africologist. It is important to underscore the fact that these terms are very problematic as the term "dialect" has a pejorative connotation and "creole" is derived from Eurocentric analysis of African phenomena. Dialectologists are those linguists who study Afro-American varieties of English, indentifying the similarities that they share with features descended from Irish-English and Scots-Irish varieties. Another school of thought about the historical development of Afro-American varieties of English is based on creole hypothesis. These linguists produce evidence which indicates African continuities or creole commonalities among Afro-American varieties which draw most of their vocabularies from European languages. There are different schools of creolists and dialectologists; but overall, all agree that such language varieties are a mixture of European languages, surviving African patterns, and contemporary innovations.

4 Debose, 1992, offers a discussion of this topic. See also John Rickford (1979). Variation in a creole Continuum: Quantitative and Implicational Approaches. Dissertation. University of Pennsylvania.

5 M. Asante (1974). A Metatheory for Black Communication. Paper presented at the Annual Meeting of the New York State Speech Association (Loch Sheldrake, April, 1974). ERIC Document ED 099945.

6 Some examples would be Lil John and the East Side Boyz' "Don't Fuck Wit Me" (Kings of Crunk); Gangsta Boo's "Life in the Metro" (Enquiring Minds); Slim Thug's "Click Clack" (Already Platinum); David Banner's "Ain't Got Nuthin" (Certified).

7 http://www.rapnewsdirect.com/News/0-202-257306-00.html#.

8 See, for example, segment on Southern American speech in the *American Tongues* video on American language varieties.

2 Crosscultural vibrations

1 For example, Rickford, 1998; Smitherman, 1987/2000; Holm, 1984; Alleyne, 1980; Bailey, 1965.

2 For example, Abrahams, 1983; Herskovits, 1941; Hurston, 1938/1990.

3 For example, Brathwaite, 1993; Cooper, 2004; Chang, 2005; Hebdige, 1987.

4 I have consulted African American and Jamaican youths in Cleveland, Ohio, and New York and Jamaican youths in Kingston and Hanover, Jamaica, to incorporate their views as participants in Hiphop, Dancehall or both. The Appendix contains examples from lyrics and definitions from authoritative sources, both literary and human.

5 Chief among them were Smitherman, 2000; Morgan, 2001; Patrick, 1995; Cassidy and LePage, 2002; Pollard, 1986; Watson, 1991; Hiphop magazines—*The Source* and *VIBE*; Jamaican Dancehall/reggae websites; Hiphop websites. In some cases, the origins of certain words or phrases were difficult to identify as Jamaican or African American innovations, as they were not listed in any of the sources. In such cases, I relied heavily on my Dancehall and Hiphop consultants and my own intuition as a Jamerican, a person of Jamaican parentage, native to America.

6 Contrary to the definition given by Wikipedia, "yardie" does not necessarily mean Jamaican criminal gang member. That usage may be local to the UK. In Jamaica, Yardie is used to refer generically to any person of Jamaican descent, whether or not they've traveled inter/outernationally.

7 There are several books that detail this history, such as Chang, 2005; Fernando, 1994; and Toop, 1992.

8 British dialects, regional varieties of English, as well as Native American languages were also available language inputs in what became America that may have influenced the speech of enslaved Africans and their descendants.

9 Cassidy and Le Page, 2002; Bailey, 1966. Roberts (2002) asserts that in the seventeenth century, the majority of enslaved African people were from the area between Senegal and Sierra Leone. In the eighteenth century, the majority were from the area of modern Liberia to Nigeria. Lalla and D'Costa (1990: 14), relying on Rawley's *The Transatlantic Slave Trade* (1981), report that "in the first half of the sixteenth century, a majority of slaves came from the area between Senegal and Sierra Leone. In the latter part of the century as many as half came from there, about a third came from Congo-Angola, and the remainder came from the Slave and Gold coasts."

10 The only similar form that I am aware of is the "gwine" pronunciation for "goin"—it seems the [ai] was productive in nineteenth–mid-twentieth-century rural Southern speech. /Bwai/ seems more phonological than lexical if we consider the forward vowel shift. However, no source that I was able to consult considers /bwai/ to be an independent U.S. Southern development. If future research found evidence of this, such would count toward the creole origins hypothesis of African American Language (AAL).

11 There are more West African-influenced language patterns than I have indicated, but I have listed only those uncovered in my data.

12 As described on the *Rebel Music* (2001) DVD.

3 Young women and critical Hiphop literacies

1 What I am calling the hood novel has been variously labeled "streetlife" or "ghetto lit." Such books are described as dealing with "guns, drug dealers and prostitutes." (Italie, 2003) A related genre is "Hiphop" fiction consisting of "gritty novels about life on the street, often written by black ex-cons, in which hip-hop music plays only a peripheral role." (Holt, 2003: 19) Although Hiphop aesthetics may be present in these types of books, the genre, though not nominally so, has been around long before Hiphop, with authors such as Donald Goins and Iceberg Slim telling the tales of the lives of pimps, prostitutes, drug dealers and various and sundry hustlers.

2 There is a difference between *identifying* with Hiphop and *being* Hiphop. That is the distinction I am trying to make when I say, "identify as Hiphop." It is the difference between identifying with a culture as opposed to being a practitioner or having the lived experience of the culture.

3 KRS-One is a Hiphop artist, activist, and edutainer who came on the scene with DJ Scott LaRock as part of Boogie Down Productions in the 1980s. He is known for busting socially conscious rhymes concerning the Black condition and is respected as being one of the greatest emcees of all time, from the golden era of Hiphop. He is still going strong.

4 See Chapter 2, p. 26.

5 In the following section: BE = ninteen-year-old; ED = nineteen-year-old; ET = seventeen-year-old; ER = researcher.

6 Mark Anthony Neal, Professor of Black Culture Studies, Duke University, shared his personal experience of being a Black male feminist during his presentation at the 2005 Hiphop Feminism Conference that took place at the University of Chicago.

4 Ride or Die B, Jezebel, Lil' Kim or Kimberly Jones and African American women's language and literacy practices

1 Although I see "Black" as a broader category signifying all people of sub-Saharan African descent and "African American" as the descendants of enslaved people who were born in America, I use the terms "Black" and "African American" synonymously here as a shorthand.

2 *The Elements' Staff*, March 10, 2005, "Lil' Kim Could Take the Stand," at http://www.hiphop-elements.com/article/read/4/6452/1/.

3 Lil' Kim, *Notorious K.I.M.*, Atlantic Records, 2000.

4 United States of America vs. Kimberly Jones, Monique Dopwell, 04 Cr. 340, New York, NY, March 10, 2005. Transcripts provided by Southern District Reporters.

5 United States of America vs. Kimberly Jones, Monique Dopwell, 04 Cr. 340, New York, NY, March 14, 2005, Closing Arguments. Transcripts provided by Southern District Reporters.

6 History shows, however, that artists' success also depends on whether they are seen as "current" by contemporary consumers. The KRS-One vs. Nelly battles prove this. Nelly had the corporations behind him and was known to new audiences, while KRS-One, although a legend who is still current, was portrayed by the media as too old. Thus, young audiences' perceptions are manipulated by the media. See Davey D's interview in *"Whatz Beef": A Hip-Hop Documentary on Beefs in 2002* (Gotham City Entertainment).

7 United States of America vs. Kimberly Jones, Monique Dopwell, 04 Cr. 340, New York, NY, March 10, 2005, Kimberly Jones Testimony, pp. 1517–20. Transcripts provided by Southern District Reporters.

8 *Ibid.*, p. 1524.

9 Hiphop slang for "cash."
10 United States of America vs. Kimberly Jones, Monique Dopwell, 04 Cr. 340, New York, NY, March 14, 2005, Closing Arguments, p. 1844. Transcripts provided by Southern District Court Reporters.
11 *Ibid.*, p. 1845.
12 *Ibid.*
13 *Ibid.*
14 *Ibid.*, Opening Arguments, p. 30.
15 *Ibid.*

5 "Yo mein Rap is phat wie deine Mama"

1 See Fatima El-Tayeb (2003) for an insightful study of the situation of people of German descent classified as legal foreigners even if born and raised in Germany and the history of Afro-Deutsch activism.
2 For a fuller discussion of the history of rap in Germany, see Pennay, 2001.
3 Though Rampton's study is not about AAL/Hiphop or African Americans, the conclusions he draws about self-contextualization in his work with South Asian youth, creole, and stylised Asian English apply.
4 http://www.20six.de/TFGNK/archive/2005/01/29/1gxm6fbgn6irw.htm.
5 The text is reproduced as it was taken from the web pages. I have not changed spelling or content.
6 Web participants offer a few interesting comments stemming from Eko's lyrics on the TFGNK site.
7 I am indebted to my colleague Jannis Androutsopolous for his knowledge of this topic and for turning me on to Yildiz (2004).
8 Redouble and quadruple just won't do!

6 Hiphop and video games

1 My students recommended the following games to me as being Hiphop: Grand Theft Auto Series (3, Vice City, and San Andreas); NBA Street (1, 2, and 3); Parappa the Rapper; Midnight Club (1, 2, and 3); Def Jam Vendetta and Fight for NY; True Crime; Tekken (4, 5, and Tag); Resident Evil Code Veronica; Madden Football (any year); NBA Live (any year); Gran Turismo 3. During my research for this manuscript, 50 Cent Bulletproof was scheduled for a November 2005 release. Also, Guerilla Black is featured in a game called 187 Ride or Die that was scheduled for an end-of-summer 2005 release.
2 See Kitwana's (2005: 46) conversation with Wendy Day of the Rap Coalition.
3 Def Jam Vendetta (2003). Electronic Arts Inc. Developed by AKI Corporation.
4 Levi Buchanan (2003: 25) reports that the real-world rap artists got to choose their own virtual outfits for the game.
5 I am the one who was talkin' trash, not my player-controlled agent/wrestler.
6 See "In the Game; Hip-hop Artists Changing the Face of Gaming Industry." In this article, Patti Miller asserts that the video-game industry has predominantly White male producers. One of the implications of White male production is a White male's point of view. Miller is the director of Children Now, a youth advocacy group that conducted a study of sexism, racism, and violence in video games—Glaubke, *et al.* (2001).
7 Marc Ecko, the fashion designer, makes this observation.
8 In this essay Frasca proposes a model whereby gamers could design their own games based on real-life situations and their own points of view. Others would have the ability to modify the game to inject alternate worldviews and scenarios. Frasca admits, though, that this would require programming ability on the part of players.

REFERENCES

Abrahams, R. (1970). *Deep Down in the Jungle: Negro Narrative Folklore from the Streets of Philadelphia.* Chicago, IL: Aldine Publishing.

—— (1983). *The Man-of-Words in the West Indies: Performance and the Emergence of Creole Culture.* Baltimore and London: The Johns Hopkins University Press.

Alim, H. S. (2003). We Are the Streets: African-American Language and the Strategic Construction of a Street Conscious Identity. In S. Makoni, G. Smitherman, A. Ball, and A. Spears (Eds.), *Black Linguistics: Language, Society and Politics in Africa and the Americas.* London and New York: Routledge.

—— (2004). Hip Hop Nation Language. In E. Finegan and J. Rickford (Eds.), *Language in the USA: Themes for the Twenty-first Century.* Cambridge: Cambridge University Press.

Alleyne, M. (1980). *Comparative Afro-American: An Historical-Comparative Study of English-Based Afro-American Dialects of the New World.* Ann Arbor, MI: Karoma.

American Tongues (1987). Video. Center for New American Media.

Anderson, E. (2002). The Code of the Streets. In S. Gabbidon, H. Taylor Greene, and V. Young (Eds.), *African American Classics in Criminology and Criminal Justice.* Thousand Oaks, CA, London: New Delhi: Sage Publications.

Androutsopoulos, J. (2004). Non-native English and Sub-cultural Identities in Media Discourse. In H. Sandøy (Ed.) Den Fleirspråklege Utfordringa. Oslo: Novus. (http://www.fu-berlin.de/phin/phin19/p19t1.htm)

—— Scholz, A. (2002). On the Recontextualization of Hip-hop in European Speech Communities. Available at http://hiphop.archetype.de/texte/sum1.html. Accessed on May 24, 2004.

Asante, M. (1991). African Elements in African-American English. In J.E. Holloway (Ed.), *Africanisms in American Culture.* Bloomington and Indianapolis: Indiana University Press.

Bailey, B. (1965). Toward a New Perspective in Negro English Dialectology. *American Speech* 40, pp. 171–7.

—— (1966). *Jamaican Creole Syntax: A Transformational Approach.* New York and London: Cambridge University Press.

Baker, H. (1984). *Blues, Ideology, and Afro-American Literature: A Vernacular Theory.* Chicago and London: University of Chicago Press.

Banks, A. (2006). *Race, Rhetoric, and Technology: Searching for Higher Ground.* Mahwah, NJ, and Urbana, IL: Lawrence Erlbaum Associates and National Council of Teachers of English.

Bennett, A. (1999). Hip Hop am Main: The Localization of Rap Music and Hip Hop Culture, Media. *Culture & Society* 21, pp. 77–91.

Bennett, L. (1966/1995). *Jamaica Labrish: Jamaican Dialect Poems*. Sangster's Bookstores: Jamaica.

Berns, J. and Schlobinski, P. (2003). Constructions of Identity in German Hip-Hop Culture. In J. Androutsopolous and A. Georgakopoulou (Eds.), *Discourse Constructions of Youth Identities*. The Netherlands and Philadelphia: John Benjamins.

Bernstein, M. (2001). New Census Categories Accurately Define Region's Ethnic Mix. *Cleveland Plain Dealer*. Available at http://www.cleveland.com/census/index.ssf?/census/more/10062322269997058.html. Accessed on June 2, 2005

Best, C. (2004). *Culture @ the Cutting Edge: Tracking Caribbean Popular Music*. Jamaica, Barbados, Trinadad and Tobago: University of the West Indies Press.

Blackshire-Belay, C. A. (1996). The Location of Ebonics within the Framework of the Africological Paradigm. *Journal of Black Studies* 27, pp. 5–23.

Blacksoftware.com. Black Home Video Game Trends. Accessed on September 25, 2005.

Bling Bling Added to *Oxford English Dictionary*. Available at http://www.mtv.com/news/articles/1471629/20030430/bg.jhtml?headlines=true.

Blommaert, J. (2003). Commentary: A Sociolinguistics of Globalization. *Journal of Sociolinguistics* 7(4), pp. 607–23.

Bokamba, E. G. (1988). Code-Mixing, Language Variation, and Linguistic Theory: Evidence from Bantu Languages. *Lingua* 76(1), pp. 21–62.

Boyd, S. (1997). Patterns of Incorporation of Lexemes in Language Contact: Language Typology or Sociolinguistics? In R. Guy, C. Feagin, D. Schiffrin and J. Baugh (Eds.), *Towards a Social Science of Language: Papers in Honor of William Labov*. Volume 2. Philadelphia: John Benjamins.

Brathwaite, K. (1993). *Roots*. Ann Arbor: University of Michigan.

Brodber, E. (1994). *Louisiana: A Novel*. London: New Beacon Books.

Buchanan, L. (2003). Video Games. *Chicago Tribune*, April 5. Accessed from Proquest on September 26, 2005.

Bucholz, M. (1997). Borrowed Blackness: African American Vernacular English and European American Youth Identities. Unpublished Ph.D. dissertation, University of California, Berkeley.

Bynoe, Y. (2004). *Stand & Deliver: Political Activism, Leadership, and Hip Hop Culture*. Brooklyn, NY: Soft Skull Press.

Campbell, H. (1988). *Rasta and Resistance: From Marcus Garvey to Walter Rodney*. Trenton, NJ: Africa World Press.

Carby, H. (1999). *Cultures in Babylon: Black Britain and African America*. London and New York: Verso.

Cassidy, F. G. and Le Page, R. B. (2002). *Dictionary of Jamaican English*. Second edition. Jamaica, Barbados, Trinidad and Tobago: University of the West Indies Press.

Celious, A. K. (2002). Blaxploitation Blues: How Black Women Identify with and Are Empowered by Female Performers of Hip hop Music. Unpublished Ph.D. dissertation, University of Michigan.

Chang, J. (2005). *Can't Stop Won't Stop: A History of the Hip-Hop Generation*. New York: St. Martin's Press.

Chang, K. and Chen, W. (1998). *Reggae Routes: The Story of Jamaican Music*. Kingston, Jamaica: Ian Randle Publishers.

Christie, P. (2003). *Language in Jamaica*. Kingston, Jamaica: Arawak Publications.

Chude-Sokei, L. (1997). Dread Discourse and Jamaican Sound Systems. In J. K. Adjaye and A. R. Andrews (Eds.), *Language, Rhythm and Sound: Black Popular Cultures into the Twenty-first Century*. Pittsburgh, PA: University of Pittsburgh Press.

Cooper, C. (1994). "Lyrical Gun": Metaphor and Role Play in Jamaican Dancehall Culture. *Massachusetts Review* 35(3–4), pp. 429–47.

—— (1995). *Noises in the Blood: Orality, Gender, and the "Vulgar" Body of Jamaican Popular Culture.* Durham: Duke University Press.

—— (2004). *Sound Clash: Jamaican Dancehall Culture at Large.* New York: Palgrave MacMillan.

Covell Waegner, C. (2004). Rap, Rebounds, and Rocawear: The "Darkening" of German Youth Culture. In R.-H. Heike (Ed.), *Blackening Europe: The African American Presence.* New York and London: Routledge.

"Crack." Meriam Webster's Online Dictionary. Available at http://www.m-w.com.

Crawford, C. (Ed.) (2001). *Ebonics and Language Education of African Ancestry Students.* New York and London: Sankofa World Publishers.

Cutler, C. (1997). Yorkville Crossing: A Case Study of the Influence of Hip-hop Culture on the Speech of a White Middle Class Adolescent in New York City. *University of Pennsylvania Working Papers in Linguistics* 4(1), pp. 371–97.

Dalby, D. (1970). Black through White: Patterns of Communication (First Annual Hans Wolff Memorial Lecture). Bloomington, IN: African Studies Program.

Dance, D. C. (1985). *Folklore from Contemporary Jamaicans.* Knoxville: University of Tennessee Press.

—— (2002). *From My People: 400 Years of African American Folklore.* New York and London: W. W. Norton.

Davis, T. (2004). The Height of Disrespect: New Study on "Hip-hop" Sexuality Finds Anti-Woman Strain—Even Among Young Women. *Village Voice*, March 17–23. Available at http://www.villagevoice.com. Accessed on October 9, 2005.

Debose, C. (1992). Codeswitching: Black English and Standard English in the African-American Linguistic Repertoire. *Journal of Multilingual and Multicultural Development* 13(1–2), pp. 157–67.

—— (2001). The Status of Variety X in the African American Linguistic Repertoire. Paper given at the New Ways of Analyzing Variation in English (NWAVE) Conference, October.

Devonish, H. (1996). Kom Groun Jamiekan Daans Haal Liricks: Memba Se A Plie Wi A Plie/Contextualizing Jamaican "Dance Hall" Music: Jamaican Language at Play in a Speech Event. *English World-Wide* 17(2), 213–37.

Dyson, M. (2001). *Holler if You Hear Me: Searching for Tupac Shakur.* New York: Basic Civitas Books/Perseus Books Group.

Eckert, P. (2000). *Linguistic Variation as Social Practice.* Malden, MA, and Oxford: Blackwell Publishers.

Edmonds, E. (1998). Dread "I" In-a Babylon: Ideological Resistance and Cultural Revitalization. In Nathaniel Murrell *et al.* (Eds.), *The Rastafari Reader: Chanting Down Babylon.* Philadelphia, PA: Temple University Press.

El-Tayeb, F. (2003). "If You Can't Pronounce My Name, You Can Just Call Me Pride": Afro German Activism, Gender and Hip Hop. *Gender & History* 15(3), November, pp. 460–86.

Encyclopedia of Hip Hop Slang. Available at http://www.nationmaster.com/encyclopedia/Hip-hop-slang.

Fairclough, N. and Chouliaraki, L. (1999). *Discourse in Late Modernity.* Edinburgh: Edinburgh University Press.

Fernando, S. H. Jr. (1994*). The New Beats: Exploring the Music, Culture, and Attitudes of Hip-hop.* New York: Anchor/Doubleday.

Fishman, J. (1997). Language, Ethnicity, and Racism. In N. Coupland and A. Jaworski (Eds.), *Sociolinguistics: A Reader*. New York: St. Martin's Press.

"Float" (1997). In *Webster's New World College Dictionary*. Third edition. New York: Simon & Schuster Macmillan Company.

Food of Jamaica. Available at http://www.jamaicans.com/tourist/overview/eating-2.shtml.

Fordham, S. (1996). *Blacked Out: Dilemmas of Race, Identity, and Success at Capital High*. Chicago, IL and London: University of Chicago Press.

Forman, M. (2002). *The Hood Comes First: Race, Space and Place in Rap and Hip-Hop*. Middletown, CT: Weslyan University Press.

Francis-Jackson, C. (2002). *The Official Dancehall Dictionary: A Guide to Jamaican Dialect and Dancehall Slang*. Kingston, Jamaica: LMH Publishing.

Frasca, G. (2004). Videogames of the Oppressed: Critical Thinking, Education, Tolerance, and Other Trivial Issues, In *First Person: New Media as Story, Performance, and Game*. N. Wardrip-Fruin and P. Harrigan (Eds.), Cambridge, MA, and London: The MIT Press.

Garrelts, N. (2003). The Official Strategy Guide for Video Game Studies: A Grammar and Rhetoric of Video Games. Unpublished Ph.D. dissertation, Michigan State University.

Gates, H. L. Jr. (1988). *The Signifying Monkey: A Theory of Afro American Literary Criticism*. New York: Harvard University Press.

Gee, J. (1996). *Social Linguistics and Literacies: Ideology in Discourses*. London and Bristol, PA: Taylor & Francis.

—— (1999). *An Introduction to Discourse Analysis: Theory and Method*. New York and London: Routledge.

—— (2000). Teenagers in New Times: A New Literacy Studies Perspective. *Journal of Adolescent and Adult Literacy* 43(5), pp. 412–20.

—— (2003). *What Video Games Have to Teach Us about Learning and Literacy*. New York and London: Palgrave Macmillan.

Gilyard, K. and Wardi, A. (2004). Folklore. In *idem, African American Literature*. New York: Longman.

Glaubke, C.R., Miller, P., McCrae, A., and Espejo, E. (2001). Fair Play? Violence, Gender and Race in Video Games. Children Now, Oakland, CA. Available as an ERIC Document, ED 463 092.

Goody, J. and Watt, I. (1968). The Consequences of Literacy. In J. Goody (Ed.), *Literacy in Traditional Societies*. New York: Cambridge University Press.

Gwinn, E. (2004). If You Play "San Andreas," You'll Be a Black Male. Does it Matter?. *Chicago Tribune*, November 1. Accessed from Proquest on September 26, 2005.

Hall, P. A. (1997). African-American Music: Dynamics of Appropriation and Innovation. In B. Ziff and P. Rao (Eds.), *Borrowed Power*. New Brunswick, NJ: Rutgers University Press.

Halliday, M. A. K. (1978). *Language as a Social Semiotic*. Baltimore, MD: University Park Press.

Hazzard-Gordon, K. (1990). *Jookin': The Rise of Social Dance Formations in African-American Culture*. Philadelphia, PA: Temple University Press.

Hebdige, D. (1987). *Cut'n'Mix: Culture, Identity, and Caribbean Music*. London: Comedia.

Herskovits, M. (1941). *Myth of the Negro Past*. New York: Harper and Brothers.

Hetata, Sherif. (1998) Dollarization, Fragmentation, and God. In F. Jameson and M. Miyoshi (Eds.), *The Cultures of Globalization*. Durham, NC, and London: Duke University Press.

Hill-Collins, P. (2004). *Black Sexual Politics: African Americans, Gender, and the New Racism*. New York and London: Routledge.

131

Holm, J. (1984). Variability of the Copula in Black English and Its Creole Kin. *American Speech* 59, pp. 291–309.

Holt, K. (2003). Fiction's Fresh Beats; Streetwise Fiction Turns a Corner, with a Fistful of Novels about Hip-Hop Music Scene. *Publishers Weekly*, September 2.

hooks, b. (1981). *Ain't I a Woman: Black Women and Feminism*. Boston: South End Press.

—— (1992). *Black Looks: Race and Representation*. Boston: South End Press.

Houston, M. (1985). Language and Black Women's Place: Evidence from the Black Middle Class. In P. Treichler, C. Kramarae and B. Stafford (Eds.), *For Alma Mater: Theory and Practice in Feminist Scholarship*. Urbana, IL: University of Illinois Press.

Hurston, Z. N. (1938/1990). *Tell My Horse: Voodoo and Life in Haiti and Jamaica*. New York: Perennial Library, Harper & Row.

Hull, G. and Nelson, M. E. (2005). Locating the Semiotic Power of Multimodality. *Written Communication* 22(2), April, pp. 224–61.

Ibrahim, A. (2003). "Whassup, homeboy?" Joining the African Diaspora: Black English as a Symbolic Site of Identification and Language Learning. In S. Makoni, G. Smitherman, A. Ball and A. Spears (Eds.), *Black Linguistics: Language, Society and Politics in Africa and the Americas*. New York and London: Routledge.

In the Game; Hip-hop Artists Changing the Face of Gaming Industry. (2005). *Chicago Tribune*, June 16. Accessed from Proquest on September 26, 2005.

Italie, H. (2003). Fast Growing Book Genre Dubbed "Street Life" Attracting Young Readers. Associated Press, May 20.

Jemie, O. (Ed.) (2003). *Yo' Mama!: New Raps, Toasts, Dozens, Jokes, and Children's Rhymes from Urban Black America*. Philadelphia, PA: Temple University Press.

Jones, V. (2005). Meet Hip-Hop's New Players: Rappers and Graffiti Artists Bring a Different Rhythm to the Video Game Industry. *Boston Globe*, June 8. Accessed from Proquest on September 22, 2005.

Kaya, A. (2001). *Sicher in Kreuzberg: Constructing Diasporas: Turkish Hip-Hop Youth in Berlin*. New Brunswick, NJ and London: Transaction Publishers.

—— (2002). Aesthetics of Diaspora: Contemporary Minstrels in Turkish Berlin. *Journal of Ethnic and Migration Studies* 28(1), pp. 43–62.

Kelley, R. D. G. (1992). Notes on Deconstructing the "Folk." *American Historical Review*, 97(5), pp. 1400–8.

—— (2002). *Freedom Dreams: The Black Radical Imagination*. Boston, MA: Beacon Press.

Kennedy, R. (2002). *Nigger: The Strange Career of a Troublesome Word*. New York: Vintage Books/Random House.

Keyes, C. (2002). *Rap Music and Street Consciousness*. Chicago and Urbana: University of Illinois Press.

Kitwana, B. (2005). *Why White Kids Love Hip Hop: Wankstas, Wiggers, Wannabes, and the New Reality of Race in America*. New York: Basic Civitas.

KRS-One. (1999). Keynote address at Hip-Hop: A Cultural Expression Conference, Cleveland State University and the Rock and Roll Hall of Fame, Cleveland, Ohio, September 14.

Kuykendall, R. A. (2002). African Blood Brotherhood, Independent Marxist during the Harlem Renaissance. *Western Journal of Black Studies* 26(1), pp. 16–21.

Lalla, B. and D'Costa, J. (1990). *Language in Exile: Three Hundred Years of Jamaican Creole*. Tuscaloosa and London: University of Alabama Press.

Lil' Kim Could Take the Stand. *The Elements*. Available at http://www.hiphop-elements.com/article/read/4/6452/1/.

Lott, E. (1996). Blackface and Blackness: the Minstrel Show in American Culture. In A. Bean, J. Hatch and B. McNamara (Eds.), *Inside the Minstrel Mask: Readings in Nineteenth-Century Blackface Minstrelsy*. Hanover, IN, and London: Wesleyan University Press.

Lubiano, W. (1997). Introduction. In W. Lubiano (Ed.), *The House that Race Built: Black Americans*. New York: Pantheon Books.

Major, C. (1970/1994). *Juba to Jive: A Dictionary of African-American Slang*. Harmondsworth: Penguin Books.

Makoni, S. and Pennycook, A. (forthcoming). *Disinventing and Constituting Language*. Clevedon: Multilingual Matters.

Makoni, S., Smitherman, G., Ball, A. and Spears, A. K. (Eds.) (2003) *Black Linguistics: Language, Society, and Politics in Africa and the Americas*. New York and London: Routledge.

Malkin, M. (2003). Hip Hop Hogwash in the Schools. Available at http://www.vdare.com/malkin/hiphop.htm. Accessed on November 14, 2005.

Marr, J. (2001). *Rebel Music: The Bob Marley Story*. DVD Palm Pictures.

Mars, P. (2004). Caribbean Influences in African-American Political Struggles, *Ethnic and Racial Studies* 27(4), pp. 565–83.

Marshall, A. (2005). The Game Boyz. *New York Times Magazine* 27, Spring.

Matthews, A. (2005). U.S. v. Lil' Kim: And Then What? *XXL: Hip-Hop on a Higher Level* 9(6), pp. 110–16.

Maultsby, P. (1991). Africanisms in African American Music. In J. Holloway (Ed.), *Africanisms in American Culture*. Bloomington: Indiana University Press.

Mintz, S. and Price, R. (1992). *The Birth of African-American Culture: An Anthropological Perspective*. Boston, MA: Beacon Press.

Mitchell, Tony (ed.) (2001). *Global Noise: Rap and Hip-Hop Outside the USA*. Middletown, CT: Wesleyan University Press.

Mitchell-Kernan, C. (1974). *Language Behavior in a Black Urban Community*. Revised edition. Berkeley, CA: University of California Berkeley, Language Behavior Research Laboratory.

—— (1988). Signifying. In H. L. Gates Jr. (1988). *The Signifying Monkey: A Theory of Afro American Literary Criticism*. New York: Harvard University Press.

Morgan, M. (1994). The African American Speech Community: Reality and Sociolinguistics. In M. Morgan (Ed.), *Language and the Social Construction of Identity in Creole Situations*. Los Angeles: Center for Afro-American Studies, UCLS.

—— (2001). "Nuthin but a G Thang": Grammar and Language Ideology in Hiphop Identity. In S. Lanehart (Ed.), *Sociocultural and Historical Contexts of African American English*. Philadelphia and London: John Benjamins.

—— (2002). *Language, Discourse and Power in African American Culture*. Cambridge: Cambridge University Press.

Myers-Scotton, C. (2002). *Contact Linguistics: Bilingual Encounters and Grammatical Outcomes*. Oxford and New York: Oxford University Press.

Neal, M. A. (2005). Black Male Feminist. Panel presentation, Hip Hop and Feminism Conference, University of Chicago, IL: April 7–9.

—— (2005) *New Black Man*. New York: Routledge.

Negus, K. (2004). The Business of Rap: Between the Street and the Executive Suite. In M. Forman and N. A. Neal (Eds.), *That's the Joint!: The Hip-Hop Studies Reader*. New York and London: Routledge.

Niaah, J. (2003). Poverty (Lab)Oratory: Rastafari and Cultural Studies. *Cultural Studies* 17(6), pp. 823–42.

Ong, W. (1982/2002). *Orality and Literacy: The Technologizing of the Word*. New York and London: Routledge.

Patrick, P. (1995). Recent Jamaican Words in Context. *American Speech* 70(3), pp. 227–64.

Pennay, M. (2001). Rap in Germany. In Tony Mitchell (Ed.), *Global Noise: Rap and Hip-Hop Outside the USA*. Middletown, CT: Wesleyan University Press.

Pennycook, A. (2003). Global Englishes, Rip Slyme, and Performativity, *Journal of Sociolinguistics* 7(4), pp. 513–33.

Pereira, J. (1998). Africanist Ideology in Jamaican Popular Music. Paper presented to the Conference on Caribbean Intellectual Traditions, University of the West Indies, Mona, November.

Perrow, E. C. (1915). Shuck Corn. *Journal of American Folk-lore* 28, p. 139.

Perry, I. (2004). *Prophets of the Hood: Politics and Poetics in Hip Hop*. Durham, NC and London: Duke University Press.

Pollard, V. (1986). Innovation in Jamaican Creole: The Speech of Rastafari. In M. Gorlach and J. Holm (Eds.), *Focus on the Caribbean*. Amsterdam and Philadelphia: John Benjamins.

—— (2000). *Dread Talk: The Language of Rastafari*. Barbados, Jamaica, Trinidad and Tobago: Canoe Press; and Montreal, Kingston, London, and Ithaca: McGill-Queen's University Press.

Pough, G. (2004). *Check It While I Wreck It: Black Womanhood, Hip-Hop Culture and the Public Sphere*. Boston, MA: Northeastern University Press.

Prahlad, Sw. A. (2001). *Reggae Wisdom: Proverbs in Jamaican Music*. Jackson: University Press of Mississippi.

Rampton, B. (1995). *Crossing: Language and Ethnicity among Adolescents*. Harlow: Longman.

—— (1999) Styling the Other: Introduction. *Journal of Sociolinguistics* 3(4), pp. 421–7.

Rap Dictionary. Available at http://www.rapdict.org.

Rasta Patois Dictionary. Available at http://www.ibpc.fr/~dror/rastadror.html

Richardson, E. (2003). *African American Literacies*. New York and London: Routledge.

—— and Lewis, S. (2000) "Flippin the Script/Blowin up the Spot": Puttin Hip Hop On-Line in (African) America and South Africa. In C. Selfe and G. Hawisher (Eds.), *Global Literacies*. New York and London: Routledge.

Rickford, J. (1987). *Dimensions of a Creole Continuum*. Stanford: Stanford University Press.

—— (1998). The Creole Origins of African-American Vernacular English: Evidence from Copula Absence. In S. Mufwene, J. Rickford, G. Bailey and J. Baugh (Eds.), *African-American English: Structure, History and Use*. New York and London: Routledge.

—— (1999). *African American Vernacular English: Features, Evolution, Educational Implications*. Massachusetts and Oxford: Blackwell.

Rickford, J. R. and Rickford, R. J. (2000). *Spoken Soul: The Story of Black English*. New York: John Wiley & Sons.

Roberts, J. W. (1989). *From Trickster to Badman: The Black Folk Hero in Slavery and Freedom*. Philadelphia: University of Pennsylvania Press.

Roberts, P. (2002). *West Indians & Their Language*. Cambridge and New York: Cambridge University Press.

Robinson, B. (1990). Africanisms in the Study of Folklore. In J. Holloway (Ed.), *Africanisms in American Culture*. Bloomington and Indianapolis: Indiana University Press.

Rose, T. (1994a). A Style Nobody Can Deal with: Politics, Style and the Postindustrial City in Hip Hop. In T. Rose and A. Rose (Eds.) *Microphone Fiends: Youth Music and Youth Culture*. New York and London: Routledge, pp. 71–85.

—— (1994b). *Black Noise: Rap Music and Black Culture in Contemporary America*. Hanover, NH: University Press of New England.

Scott, C. D. (2000). Crossing Cultural Borders: Girl and Look as Markers of Identity in Black Women's Language Use. *Discourse & Society* 11(2), pp. 237–48.

Sebeok, T. (2001). *Global Semiotics*. Bloomington and Indianapolis: Indiana University Press.

Sharpe, J. (2003). Cartographies of Globalization, Technologies of Gendered Subjectivities: The Dub Poetry of Jean "Binta" Breeze. *Gender & History*, 15(3), pp. 440–59.

Skinner, E. (2001). Empirical Research on Mass Communication and Cultural Domination in the Caribbean. In H. A. Regis (Ed.), *Culture and Mass Communication in the Caribbean*. Gainesville: University Press of Florida.

Slanguistics. (2004). An MTV2 production.

Smitherman, G. (1977/1986). *Talkin and Testifyin: The Language of Black America*. Boston: Houghton Mifflin; reissued, with revisions, Detroit, MI: Wayne State University Press.

—— (1987/2000). *Talkin that Talk: Language, Culture and Education in African America*. New York and London: Routledge.

—— (1994). *Black Talk: Words and Phrases from the Hood to the Amen Corner*. First edition. Boston: Houghton Mifflin.

—— (1998). Word from the Hood: The Lexicon of African-American Vernacular English. In S. Mufwene, J. Rickford, G. Bailey and J. Baugh (Eds.), *African-American English: Structure, History and Use*. New York and London: Routledge.

—— (2000). *Black Talk: Words and Phrases from the Hood to the Amen Corner*. Revised edition. Boston: Houghton Mifflin.

—— (2006). *Word from the Mother: Language and African Americans*. New York and London: Routledge.

Souljah, (1999). *The Coldest Winter Ever*. New York: Pocket Books.

Southern Rap. Available at http://www.rapnewsdirect.com/News/0-202-257306-00.html#.

Spady, J. G. and Eure, J. D. (1991). *Nation Conscious Rap*. New York and Philadelphia, PA: PC International Press.

Spina, S. (2004). Power Plays: Video Games' Bad Rap. In S. Steinberg and J. Kincheloe (Eds.), *Kinderculture: The Corporate Construction of Childhood*. Second edition. Boulder, CO: Westview Press.

Stanley-Niaah, S. (2004). Kingston's Dancehall. *Space & Culture* 7(1), February, pp. 102–18.

Stolzoff, N. (2000). *Wake the Town and Tell the People: Dancehall Culture in Jamaica*. Durham, NC: Duke University Press.

Street, B. (1994). What Is Meant by "Local Literacies"? In D. Barton (Ed.), *Sustaining Local Literacies*. Clevedon: Multilingual Matters.

Thug Life: Videogame Publishers Think You're Street—and They Want You to Think They Are Too. (2004). *Official U.S. Playstation Magazine* 83, August 1. Accessed from Proquest on September 22, 2005.

Toop, D. (1997). *Rap Attack 2: African Rap to Global Hip Hop*. Serpent's Tail. Revised edition. London: Serpent's Tail.

Tribbett-Williams, L. A. (2000). Saying Nothing, Talking Loud: Lil' Kim and Foxy Brown, Caricatures of African American Womanhood. *Southern California Review of Law and Women's Studies* 10, pp. 167–207.

Troutman, D. (2001). African American Women: Talking that Talk. In S. Lanehart (Ed.), *Sociocultural and Historical Contexts of African American Vernacular English*. Philadelphia, PA: John Benjamins.

135

T'sou, B. K. (1975). On the Linguistic Covariants of Cultural Assimilation. *Anthropological Linguistics* 17(9), pp. 445–65.

Turner, L. D. (1969). *Africanisms in the Gullah Dialect*. New York: Arno Press and the New York Times.

van Dijk, T. (1993). *Elite Discourse and Racism*. Newbury Park, CA: Sage Publications.

—— (2001). Critical Discourse Analysis. In D. Schriffin, D. Tannen and E. Hamilton (Eds.), *The Handbook of Discourse Analysis*. Malden, MA: Blackwell.

Vibe (2004). August.

Warner, C. R. (1993). Jah as Genre: The Interface of Reggae and American Popular Music. Unpublished dissertation, Bowling Green State University.

Watson, G. L. (1991). *Jamaican Sayings: With Notes on Folklore, Aesthetics, and Social Control*. Gainesville, FL: Florida A&M University Press.

Weinreich, U. (1968/1974). *Languages in Contact: Findings and Problems*. Eighth edition. The Hague: Mouton Co. N. V. Publishers.

Williams, J. (n.d.). *Original Dancehall Dictionary*. Third edition. Yard Productions.

Williams, R. L. (1975). *Ebonics: The True Language of Black Folks*. St. Louis, MO: Institute of Black Studies.

Williamson Nelson, L. (1990) Code-Switching in the Oral Life Narratives of African-American Women: Challenges to Linguistic Hegemony. *Journal of Education* 172(3), pp. 142–55.

Yarbrough, M. and Bennett, C. (2000). Cassandra and the "Sistahs": The Peculiar Treatment of African American Women in the Myth of Women as Liars. *Journal of Gender, Race and Justice* 3(2), pp. 625–57.

Yildiz, Y. (2004). Critically "Kanak": A Reimagination of German Culture. In A. Gardt and B. Hüppauf (Eds.), *Globalization and the Future of German*. Berlin and New York: Mouton deGruyter.

Zips, W. (1995). "Let's Talk about the Motherland": Jamaican Influences on the African Discourses of the Diaspora. In W. Hoogbergen (Ed.), *Born out of Resistance: On Caribbean Cultural Creativity*. Utrecht: ISOR.

German website references

http://www.20six.de/weblogCategory/117es50ayrlnu?d=29.1.2005
http://www.ard.de/intern/index_view.phtml?k2=4andk3=7andk4=1
http://www.chart-radio.de/viewartistbio.php3?interpret=eko+fresh
http://www.HiphopLyrics.de
http://www.ksavas.de/ksavas/lyrics/lyrics.htm
http://www.mtvhome.de/hitlistgermany/index.php
http://www.mzee.com/forum/showthread.php?threadid=103925
http://www.rap.de
http://www.rheimland.de
http://www.20six.de/TFGNK/archive/2005/01/29/1gxm6fbgn6irw.htm

INDEX